T0131231

The Old Way North

THE
Following the
OLD
Oberholtzer–Magee
WAY
Expedition
NORTH

DAVID F. PELLY

**BOREALIS
BOOKS**

Borealis Books is an imprint of the Minnesota Historical Society Press.

www.borealisbooks.org

© 2008 by David F. Pelly. All rights reserved. No part of this book may be used or reproduced in any manner whatsoever without written permission, except in the case of brief quotations embodied in critical articles and reviews. For information, write to Borealis Books, 345 Kellogg Blvd. W., St. Paul, MN 55102-1906.

The Minnesota Historical Society Press is a member of the Association of American University Presses.

Manufactured in the United States of America

10 9 8 7 6 5 4 3 2 1

∞ The paper used in this publication meets the minimum requirements of the American National Standard for Information Sciences—Permanence for Printed Library Materials, ANSI Z39.48-1984.

International Standard Book Number
ISBN 13: 978-0-87351-616-7 (cloth)
ISBN 10: 0-87351-616-8 (cloth)

Library of Congress
Cataloging-in-Publication Data
Pelly, David F., 1948–
The old way North : following the Oberholtzer-Magee expedition / David F. Pelly.
    p.   cm.
Includes bibliographical references and index.
ISBN-13: 978-0-87351-616-7
    (cloth : alk. paper)
ISBN-10: 0-87351-616-8
    (cloth : alk. paper)
  1. Manitoba—Description and travel.
  2. Hudson Bay Region—Description and travel.
  3. Oberholtzer, Ernest C. (Ernest Carl), 1884–1977—Travel—Manitoba
  4. Magee, Billy—Travel—Manitoba.
  5. Pelly, David F., 1948– —Travel—Manitoba.
  6. Oberholtzer, Ernest C. (Ernest Carl), 1884–1977—Diaries.
  7. Frontier and pioneer life—Manitoba
  8. Canoes and canoeing—Manitoba—History—20th century.
  9. Chipewyan Indians—History—20th century.
  10. Cree Indians—History—20th century.
  I. Title.

F1063.P45 2008
917.127′1042—dc22
                              2008004806

To Jean Sandford Replinger,
a modern visionary of the wilderness,
with eternal admiration and gratitude

Contents

Preface

Most people know something of the early search for the North-west Passage by sea from the North Atlantic and its role in mapping and exploring the northern reaches of Canada. Similarly, northern history buffs are quite familiar with the overland route used by Alexander Mackenzie, John Franklin, George Back, and many others: from Edmonton north to Athabasca, down the Slave River to Great Slave Lake, the Mackenzie River itself, and other points beyond. But the central travel corridor into what remains today the heart of Canada's northern wilderness—from Manitoba to the vast stretch of Nunavut on the west side of Hudson Bay—remains shrouded in mystery, its natural and cultural history largely ignored. All three of these northern travel routes, and their respective histories, are a function of geography: two of them we know well, and understand why; the third is perhaps unjustly uncelebrated.

While most readers know about Sir John Franklin, and many know of Samuel Hearne, few know the names of those intrepid travelers who explored the inland northern waterways by canoe: A. P. Low, Guy Blanchet, and J. B. Tyrrell, among others. Although the canoe is a Canadian icon, for some strange reason the hardy individuals who used it to first penetrate the unexplored (by white men) reaches of this country did not capture the public's imagination in a lasting way. Yet could anyone imagine a more difficult challenge than to endure weeks of paddling, facing the elements with only the crudest of shelter—it was a life of labor, skill, and deprivation and of wind and bugs, often with no certainty of success or even survival.

Though Ernest C. Oberholtzer was neither of this set nor their equal, he did travel in their wake, and he did so in the earliest days of recreational canoeing in Canada. He therefore offers us an unusual link back in time. What fascinates me most is that he followed a particular old travel route to the North, one that touches many diverse elements of Canadian history and that dates back with certainty to before the arrival of Europeans, and yet was heavily used well into the twentieth century. Oberholtzer offers us our window into this past. Explorers, mapmakers, geologists, fur traders, trappers, Mounties, missionaries, and before all of them, the Native people themselves all used this travel corridor extensively. This book is the story that land could tell.

I am a canoeist. Over the past thirty years, I have paddled thousands of miles on rivers and lakes in northern Canada—it has been a central theme to my life. That I felt some sense of empathy with Ernest Oberholtzer should not have surprised me. He went on his 1912 epic canoe trip to the North at age twenty-eight; at twenty-nine I took my first canoe trip in the Arctic. (One difference is that I've been back many times, in most years since.) Both of us were changed, for life. We both became fascinated with the Native cultures of the North. We both went on to collect oral histories and traditional knowledge from these cultures. In our own ways, we both became storytellers. We both developed an attachment to the land that in turn defined our lives. The northern landscape has been one of my closest companions on the journey of life. There is no question the land has left its impression on me. It tells stories; I listen. At times, I am stirred to write them down, and this is one such occasion.

I would not have been able to do so, however, without the collaboration of Lynda Holland and Bill Layman. These two, who live in northern Saskatchewan, who have worked among the Dene (Chipewyan) for years and who typically spend their summers canoeing one portion or another of the old way North, were facilitators of the first order for this project. They searched archives; they mined oral histories; they shared their insights into the region and the people; and they opened doors for me when we visited the Dene communities through which Oberholtzer's route passed. Much of the credit for this book's wealth of story goes to these two friends, though any errors or misjudgements remain entirely my responsibility.

Finally, there are some important details to share regarding the actual words you will read. Several period documents are quoted verbatim. Wherever possible, the spelling mistakes and grammatical errors of the original have been retained (unless to do so would create confusion) in order to preserve the full flavor of the writer's prose. Excerpts from Oberholtzer's 1912 trip journal are shown in italics.

In the interest of clarity for readers on both sides of the border, I have used the term "Native" when referring to those aboriginal people whom, in Canada, we call the First Nations. Most particularly, in this context, this includes, with utmost respect, the Cree and Dene (Chipewyan). It is an essential truth that for these people above all, those who are most profoundly native to this landscape, the corridor at the heart of this book was first their way North.

D.F.P
"Kipawa"
Feby 2008

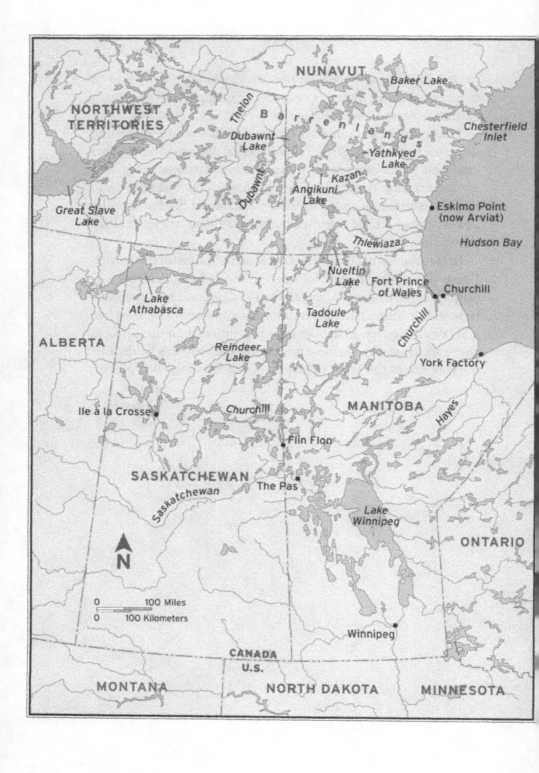

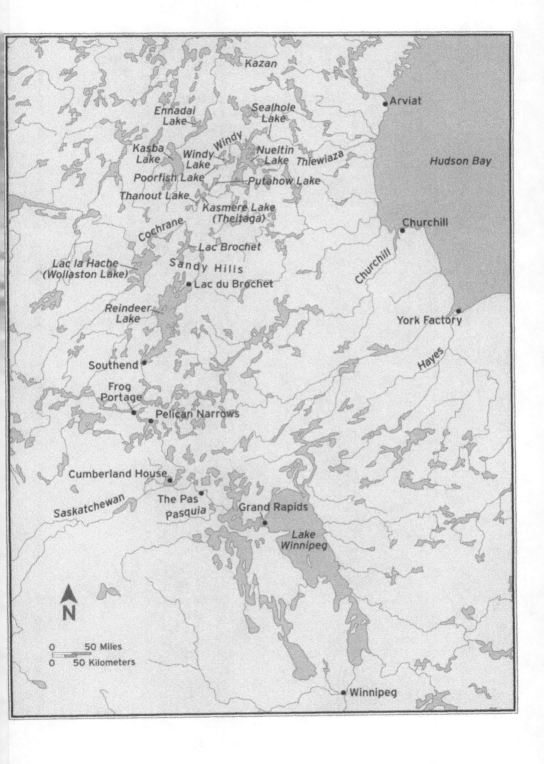

Acknowledgments

Research for this book was a lengthy and expensive process, made possible by generous financial support from Barbara Garner, especially, through the Ernest C. Oberholtzer Foundation of Minnesota, and numerous other individuals who contributed in memory of Ober's friends: Ted and Rody Hall, Fritz Hilke, Frank Hubachek, Charles Scott Kelly, Gene Ritchie Monahan, and Fredrick and Donald Winston. Also from the Quetico Foundation of Toronto and their donors, including the McLean Foundation, Andrew M. Stewart, William "Sarge" Sargent, and Jean Sanford Replinger.

The actual writing of this book was supported by a generous grant from the Canada Council for the Arts.

Quotes from the Oberholtzer documents held at the Minnesota Historical Society—his trip journals, correspondence, notebooks, and oral history interviews—are used with permission of the Ernest C. Oberholtzer Foundation.

The biographical quotes in the concluding chapter, describing Oberholtzer's contributions to wilderness preservation, are taken from the essay "A Very Able Fellow" in *Toward Magnetic North,* used here with permission of the Oberholtzer Foundation.

Quotes in the chapters entitled "Memories," "Nu-thel-tin-tua, Qikiqtariaktuk," and "Dene Reflections," from Julien Toulejour, Leon Medal, and Jimmy Dzeylion, respectively, as well as other valuable insights into Dene history, were taken from the two-volume record of the Dene Elders Project (Holland-Dalby Educational Consulting, 2002 and 2003), used with permission of the editor, Lynda Holland.

The excerpts from Brother Celestin Guillet's journal are reproduced with permission of the Oblate Archives, Grandin Province, as provided by archivist Diane Lamoreux, who was extremely helpful with this work.

The *Codex historicus du Lac Caribou* is excerpted with permission of the Centre du Patrimoine, St. Boniface, Manitoba.

In addition to personal interviews with Philomene Umpherville, in April 2005, the section of the chapter entitled "Memories" about Philomene Umpherville's family is based on a master's thesis by Michelle Tracy entitled "A Bead Box of My Own." The author is grateful for permission to draw upon her excellent and comprehensive work.

Many insights into the life and character of Ernest Oberholtzer were revealed in the fine biography of the man, *Keeper of the Wild*, by Joe Paddock, who also assisted most ably with research at the Minnesota Historical Society.

Work on this project, from its inception, was guided—both in spirit and with advice—by Bob Cockburn, who from the outset knew the stories of this land far better than I did, but nonetheless supported my pursuit.

The Old Way North

The One They Want

Looking North

"GUESS READY GO END EARTH," said Billy Magee to the fur trader at the Mine Centre post in the Rainy Lake district of northwestern Ontario. Billy, his store name—his real name was Taytáhpah-swáywetong—was a strong-looking man, about fifty, with high cheekbones and a placidly round face, wearing a black broad-brimmed hat. He habitually sold his furs in Mine Centre. As always at the trading posts of the day, the men who gathered there shared their news—it was a focal point of communication. It was no surprise then that the storekeeper that day, in the spring of 1912, was telling Billy he'd received a letter from their mutual acquaintance, a younger man by the name of Ernest Oberholtzer, proposing a long and difficult—and somewhat ill-defined—canoe trip and inviting Magee to join him. Oberholtzer asked the storekeeper to tell Billy, "We would be gone six months, at least, and that we might get frozen in and have to stay all winter, and to tell Billy that it was the hardest thing he had ever done in all his life, but that I wouldn't go without him."

The very notion of paddling so far north that they would go off the map was quite naturally akin to a trip "to the end of the Earth" in the mind of this Anishinaabe man. Nevertheless, Magee must have quite liked the young white man from far away who had issued the invitation—they had already paddled thousands of miles together in the Rainy Lake district—and presumably, he had nothing else in particular planned for the coming summer, the slow season for a trapper. So why not go on this mysterious adventure? "Guess I go. Why not?" he might have said with a slight shrug, with little idea where he was actually headed and virtually no concept of what the journey would entail.

The two first met at Mine Centre in 1909 when Oberholtzer

needed a guide for his intended paddle in the Rainy Lake district. "Now, Billy," he said, "I want to see everything. I don't care how hard it is." Thus did their mutual respect begin. "Our trip together was wholly harmonious," wrote Oberholtzer later, "and he seemed to enjoy it as much as I did." Magee, according to Oberholtzer, was such a skilled guide that "he could feel the trail under his feet, where it once had been," as they found their way through the wilderness, over long-abandoned portage trails. Years later, he said, "I saw that Billy was extremely intelligent, well-informed, industrious, and willing to do almost anything to please. . . . He was a man of few words and great modesty. You could tell that right away. And I took quite a fancy to him."

One time, when Oberholtzer impetuously threatened to engage a different guide, in a temporary fit of anger after Magee's rare Saturday night of drinking, the Anishinaabe man responded, "Guess no cry. I'm not very sorry about it. You see, you damn fool."

Ernest Oberholtzer, age twenty-eight,
and Billy Magee, age fifty, in the summer of 1912.

There was an honest tension underlying their mutual respect, it seems, requiring each to acknowledge the other's role, that was to serve them well in their expedition. "His love of the unknown like mine," wrote Oberholtzer in his notebook, later, "no place too remote or difficult."

~ ~ ~ ~ ~

Ernest Oberholtzer, in his midtwenties, having discovered the joys of travel by canoe while in the Rainy Lake district, allowed his imagination to be fueled by reading accounts of the barrenlands, principal among them the writings of J. B. Tyrrell, a geologist who was among the earliest white men to travel there. Oberholtzer dreamed of emulating his hero. "If you want to go to a place where the information you bring back will really be valuable," he said, "this is the place to go." The barrenlands of his dreams were the tundra plains north of Manitoba, Canada's youngest province at the time, having been carved out of the Northwest Territories just a few years earlier in 1906. Northern Manitoba, Saskatchewan, and Alberta were the frontier. Treaties had just been concluded with some of the Dene, whose traditional lands stretched across the top of all three new provinces.* Government land commissioners were in the process of laying down plans for settlement of these northlands. Beyond that, farther north, lay virtually unexplored wilderness, as viewed from the perspective of the white man in southern Canada or the United States. That's where Oberholtzer wanted to go.

"Tyrrell's own never-to-be-forgotten report on his exploration of the Kazan River, the vast herds of Barren Ground caribou encountered, and his discovery of a hitherto unknown band of inland Eskimos, living entirely by their own stone-age economy, had fired my imagination," wrote Oberholtzer some years later. As romantic as that call of the unknown sounds today, it was no doubt

---

* The Dene, or Chipewyan, are the Native (or First Nations) people of the Athapaskan language group whose traditional lands stretch across the top of the three provinces and north into the territories.

entirely real and genuinely mysterious in the mind of a young man searching for adventure in the early twentieth century.

Ernest Oberholtzer was born in 1884 in Iowa. His parents were divorced six years later, and his younger brother died a few months after that, leaving Ernest alone with his mother. They retreated together to live with her parents, and so Ernest grew up deeply affected by his maternal grandparents, even as the close bond to his mother grew out of the adversity. Living on the banks of the Mississippi River, young Ernest watched massive rafts of logs floating downstream to the mill and pondered "the vast unknown North" whence they came.

In 1903, Oberholtzer left home to attend Harvard, where he pursued a diversity of courses in philosophy, psychology, landscape architecture, English, and geology, while on the side contributing to Harvard's literary magazine and studying the violin under the concertmaster of the Boston Symphony. As he said, "I never learned [enough of] anything that I could earn a living with. But I found out more about myself and what my interests were." During the summer between completing his bachelor's degree and beginning his graduate studies in landscape planning, he headed to northern Minnesota for his introduction to wilderness canoeing and the Native peoples of the region. What he discovered in all of this study and experience, at its root, was an abiding interest in the land and its multiple uses, a perspective that would channel his energies through much of life. It may also explain why, just a few years later, the notion took hold of him to see the "vast unknown North"—a land where all possibilities still lay ahead.

Oberholtzer read whatever he could find: "I looked up everything there was on the Barren Lands." The earliest account came from Samuel Hearne, an English fur trader and employee of the Hudson's Bay Company (HBC), who traversed what he called the Barren Ground on foot from 1769 to 1772, accompanied by Dene guides, most significantly Matonabbee, traveler extraordinaire and a major ambassador for the fur trade among his people. On his third and successful attempt, Hearne followed Matonabbee's size-able party of hunters and women—who were necessary to cook and sew and "made for labour; one of them can carry, or haul, as much as two men can do," according to Matonabbee—from the mouth of the Churchill River on Hudson Bay, northwest to the mouth of the Coppermine River at the Arctic Ocean, and back. Hearne's account of this remarkable journey of at least two thousand miles (as the crow flies) provides readers with a first detailed glimpse of the land and its people. In a very matter-of-fact voice, he described the difficulties of his long journey and offered innumerable details of how the Indians traveling with him were able to survive in this harsh landscape. Captivating though it may have been to the young reader, Hearne's own words cannot be said to offer an enticing picture of the wilderness: "In my opinion, there cannot exist a stronger proof that mankind was not created to enjoy happiness in this world, than the conduct of the miserable beings who inhabit this wretched part of it."

A Canadian edition of Hearne's account was published in 1911, edited by J. B. Tyrrell. One need not wonder, therefore, why Oberholtzer devoured the book in all its detail and with such passion. He kept copious handwritten notes as he read, most of them related to the birds and mammals of the North or to the culture or sociology of the Dene and Inuit, or the Chipewyan and Eskimos, as he called them. Among these notes, he penned:

> Mr. Tyrrell writes: "I happen to be the only one since Hearne who has conducted explorations in the country lying between Fort Churchill and the eastern end of Great Slave Lake and south of latitude 63°N. Except Hearne, I and those who accompanied and assisted me are the only white men who have crossed that great stretch of country.... Absolutely the only information that I had about the region when I visited it, other than what I had secured in conversation with Indians, was contained in Hearne's book.... It is hardly necessary to say that a magnificent field for exploration is still left in that far northern country."

One can just imagine Oberholtzer's desire to be the next white man to enter this country after reading that.

Without doubt, he also read David Hanbury's 1904 book, *Sport and Travel in the Northland of Canada*. In 1899, thirty-five-year-old Hanbury, a well-educated British adventurer, arrived at Fort Churchill on Hudson Bay by dogsled from the south. That spring he pushed on farther north up the coast, to Chesterfield Inlet, where he turned inland. Over the next three years he traveled upstream by canoe across the barrenlands, returned downstream the following summer, overwintered among the Inuit near Baker Lake, and then traveled by sled to the Arctic coast and west to the Mackenzie River. In his book, he wrote of his first barrenlands transit: "The journey eventually turned out to be so absurdly easy, that I more than once regretted that it was so, for half the pleasure of exploration is derived from meeting and surmounting difficulties." Such bravado would have done anything but strike fear in Oberholtzer's heart as he anticipated his own expedition.

After reading Hanbury, Oberholtzer made several pages of notes, interested in particular with the author's thoughts on "the Eskimos." Hanbury wrote: "They have no account of the creation of the world and their story of the origin of the human race is incoherent." While one wonders how Hanbury came to this inaccurate conclusion, it is nonetheless noteworthy that this, of all things, fascinated Oberholtzer such that he wrote it down. In his own notebook, Oberholtzer adopted the use of the slang "Husky" when referring to Inuit, as in "A Husky thinks nothing of packing 200 pounds."

If it was Hearne who provided the earliest glimpse of life on the barrenlands for a youthful Oberholtzer, it was Tyrrell who laid out the travel route to get there. In 1894, Tyrrell's assigned task was to extend the geological map of Canada north beyond the limit of northern Manitoba, where the work had already been done. Tyrrell himself was responsible for much of the exploration and mapping of northern Manitoba and Saskatchewan during his fieldwork seasons from 1887 to 1892. In 1894, he was to leave from the most northerly outpost on Reindeer Lake, six hundred miles north of Winnipeg, and follow a route long used by the Native peoples but only once followed by a white man, a missionary, north to the barrenlands. There he would find and follow, even farther north, a large river that the Dene had described to him previously and which Hearne had crossed more than a century before. Today we know it as the Kazan, a derivative of the Chipewyan word *KacasKza* (The Place Where It Is Very, Very Cold, Where the Water Freezes in Lumps on the Willows). It was Tyrrell's account of this journey that had more than anything else, as Oberholtzer put it, fired his imagination.

Years later at age eighty, Oberholtzer reminisced about his expedition and its origins.

> I came across the work of J. B. Tyrrell, who was by all odds the greatest of all the modern geographers. A very remarkable man! ... He found, he actually found—at that late day, maybe 1897,* something like that—a tribe of Eskimos living inland that had never been known to anybody. So far as he knew, they'd never seen a white man. They were living on this Kazan River, as it was called. ... J. B. never wrote anything but his reports to the geological service. But to me it was one of the most fascinating things I had ever read in all my life. ... I had read and had been greatly impressed. The two things, of course, that meant more to me than anything else was seeing all those caribou and seeing these Eskimos that nobody had ever known. And my imagination was at work. I thought, well, there are probably other groups of those Eskimos up in there. What that would mean, what a delight to be the first one ever to find them!! ... So these things had impressed me very greatly, and I wanted to go up in there.

There can be little doubt that when he read Tyrrell's account Oberholtzer dreamed of sharing such an experience: "Below this rocky ridge, where an Eskimo grave was conspicuously marked by some tall upright pieces of wood, the river enters the upper extension of a large lake, called by the Eskimos, Angikūni Kamanyie, or

---

* The actual date was 1894.

Great Lake, doubtless the Titmeg Lake of Samuel Hearne. Many Eskimos were camped in the vicinity, and at one time our two Peterboro canoes were surrounded by twenty-three Eskimo kyacks." It was on this same lake that Tyrrell wrote:

> The party was here delayed half a day by adverse wind, during which time it was visited by an Eskimo trader, named Anuleah, who makes an annual trip to the trading store at the north end of Reindeer Lake, taking out the few furs collected by his neighbours, and bringing back tobacco, ammunition, needles, &c. He was greatly surprised to find that these white men were not traders, and would not even accept from him the skins of foxes or wolves, but to him, as to all the other natives who were met, small presents were given in token of friendship. He agreed to carry a letter to the trading store, and the letter reached Ottawa via Cumberland and Winnipeg, in safety, on March 5th 1895.

Oberholtzer, with his planned route from Winnipeg to The Pas to Cumberland to Reindeer Lake, then north to the barrenlands and the Kazan River, must have wondered if he too would meet Anuleah or his successors.

Of the land, Tyrrell painted an alluring image: "The whole landscape, seen in the early morning light, presented such a picture of wild, but quiet beauty, as I have seldom had the good fortune to enjoy." Tyrrell's map, which Oberholtzer carried, was little more than a sketch of the land and waterways to be found north of Reindeer Lake. Nonetheless, it represented the extent of mapped knowledge for the country to the north, beyond the frontier.

∽   ∽   ∽   ∽   ∽

Oberholtzer was not alone in dreaming of such far-off adventure. It was an era of public fascination with tales of adventurous travel and survival against the odds, and in the extreme, heroic failure. It's a safe bet that many young men of the time knew about Robert Peary's claim of reaching the North Pole on April 6, 1909, and pondered whether he did in fact make it, and of Roald

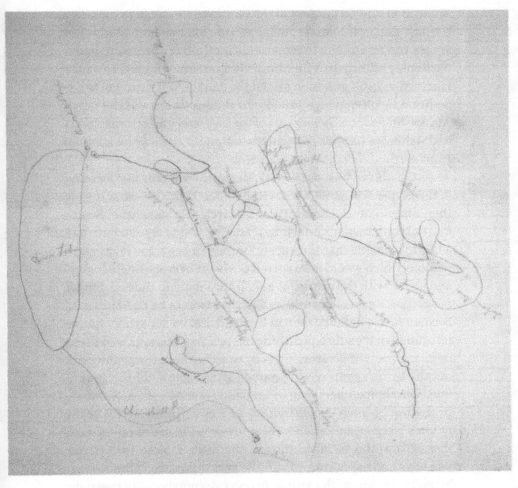

*This map was drawn for J. B. Tyrrell on July 19, 1894,
by the Chipewyan guide Savasis, better known as St. Pierre.
Even in 1912, this drawing was the full extent of the
mapped knowledge of the Thlewiaza's course to Hudson Bay.*

Amundsen's 1906 conquest of the Northwest Passage in the *Gjoa*, the first ship ever to make it through the long-sought-after route across the top of North America. Oberholtzer probably had a particular affinity to Vilhjalmur Stefansson, who left Iowa for Harvard in 1903 and then joined the Anglo-American Polar Expedition in 1906, which sailed into the Arctic around the top of Alaska. Stefansson became one of the best-known Arctic explorers and writers of his day, particularly noted for the way he adopted Inuit methods of survival and travel.

As Oberholtzer set out in 1912, the world was only just learning of the heroic deaths of Captain Robert Scott with his party during their attempt at the South Pole in March that same year. Scott's journal contained his final lines, "Had we lived I should have had a tale to tell of the hardihood, endurance and courage of my companions which would have stirred the heart of every Englishman," and ended with the words, "We shall stick it out to the end, but we are getting weaker of course and the end cannot be far." He was to become such a national hero in England that books, art, sculpture, film, and poetry subsequently developed the tragic, as well as the heroic, aspects of his story. Streets, churches, and towns throughout the British Empire were named after Scott and his companions. Oberholtzer had been in England for much of the two years preceding his own expedition, so he was certainly aware of the public's fascination for their Antarctic hero. All of this offers some insight into the social context of the time, replete with heroic journeys and expeditions into "the vast unknown." Oberholtzer longed to be part of the action. In one 1910 notebook, in the midst of various jottings about others' northern explorations, he had written (as if a "note to self"): "Possibly make an interesting historical discovery."

It seems clear that Oberholtzer wanted to position himself among the explorers and writers of the day, at least in some small way. He had made some initial forays into the field of wilderness travel writing, but this trip to "the vast unknown North" would earn him solid standing, he hoped, perhaps even approaching that of his hero J. B. Tyrrell. His notebooks offer some evidence of this aspiration. In one piece of advice to himself, he wrote: "Real stories full of zest, reality, daring, reckless, resourceful, wonderful—let the reader draw breath at the end and exclaim 'But he was a man.' Tell it cold-bloodedly, off-hand, so that it allows a picture of truth."

To foster an association with other explorers, he attended lectures by both Roald Amundsen and Vilhjalmur Stefansson, recording afterwards his favorable impressions of both men, whom he somehow contrived to meet following the lectures. He wrote to J. B. Tyrrell, to Vilhjalmur Stefansson, and to David Hanbury, all three remarkable northern travelers of the time, and to the Reverend J. Lofthouse, who later became bishop of the Arctic. Stefansson helped him with some "Eskimo" vocabulary. Tyrrell wrote back: "I shall hope to see a splendid account of your journey in one of the good magazines very soon." In his letter to Hanbury, he asked for advice and closed with, "Thanking you for the pleasure I have often had in reading of your splendid work in the north," but there is no record of a reply. Hanbury died shortly thereafter, perhaps without even receiving the letter.

Despite his notes and journals, he wrote little of his own thoughts on the proposed expedition, so it is difficult to imagine today Oberholtzer's sense of uncertainty and anticipation in preparing for such a journey into "the vast unknown North."

The Journey Begins

▷ ▷ *June 26 [, 1912]. Slight showers. I buy more supplies and visit the [HBC] factor, who said he had made a long trip the previous year to Fort Churchill where he secured a picture of a walrus. Clark [the HBC man] says there is a 'mint of money' to be made out of an article about the Split Lake [Hudson Bay] railway.*

I decide to go to Cumberland House for a man; and, after a talk with a young French candidate, we start out at 3 o'clock. Weather has become settled. A fair wind. Poplars and willows along the banks. Crows, swallows, song birds. We make good distance and camp at nine o'clock on a very muddy shore. Billy dips up muddy water with the bucket attached to a long stick. Go to bed at a quarter past ten.

With these inauspicious words, Oberholtzer begins his handwritten record of their expedition by canoe. In Davenport, Iowa, he said farewell to his mother, to whom he was so close. "My mother gave me a dollar and half watch and a dollar and a half compass, for finding my way and mapping the country," he later reminisced. "Then in early June, I came up to International Falls and went over to Fort Frances, and Billy Magee was waiting for me there."

After a week of train travel involving several legs, interspersed with shopping for supplies and enduring uncomfortable nights in various hotels along the way from Fort Frances to Winnipeg to Hudson Bay Junction to The Pas, they must have been happy to put their paddles in the muddy water and feel the canoe surge forward at the beginning of their great adventure. The "French candidate," apparently, was not suitable to serve as their guide, so the two northern novices headed off on their own, hoping to hire a guide at Cumberland House.

The Pas, where their journey really began, was the railhead at the time, the tracks having been extended there from Hudson Bay Junction just two years before. In this sense, then, this was the frontier. The railway offered a new connection to the west—from here steamboats used the river to carry goods right across the prairies to the western frontier at Edmonton. Oberholtzer observed the "piers of a new bridge" under construction over the Saskatchewan River, which must have been the beginning of the new railway line to Hudson Bay, via Split Lake, to which Oberholtzer gives passing reference in his journal.

The railway construction was clearly a significant development for the region. In his report of that spring's "dog train" patrol along the railway's cut trail from Le Pas (as it was then called), Royal North West Mounted Police* inspector H. M. Newson mentions encountering eight teams of men returning from freighting supplies up to construction camps spaced out along the trail. "The number of men at present at work is not many more than about 60, all told along the right of way. They are simply clearing the bush and consist chiefly of Swedes and Galicians [Ukrainians]." Construction camps had been established at mile ten, mile seventeen, mile twenty-seven, and mile thirty-seven along the trail, and from each one the head engineer was responsible for ten miles of the route. The route opened up the country for others as well, as Inspector Newson noted: "Two trappers [were] on their way to George Cowans who lives at camp #4, there names were Olaf Rude and Clarence Mettoon. . . . At camp #4 there are three prospectors, Ferguson, Whalley & Bancroft, who are waiting for the ice to go when they are proceeding to the vicinity of Grassey River. They have with them 4 months supplies."

Located at the junction of the Pas (or Pasquia) River with the Saskatchewan River—the water highway of the west—The Pas had long been a focal point for early travelers in the midnorthern stretch of what eventually became Manitoba. The French—the fur

---

* The Royal North West Mounted Police (RNWMP) were the precursor to today's Royal Canadian Mounted Police (RCMP). The name changed in 1920.

traders from New France—built a fort here as early as 1749, some twenty-five years before the English made their move inland from the Bay. The HBC trading post at The Pas was established in 1856, as Fort Defiance, and in 1870 the Company began operating steamboats along the deep, smooth water of the Saskatchewan. Company records refer to "taking in over 30,000 muskrats" by March of 1879; even though the sale price for muskrat was no more than a few dollars each, that represented a good income for a single winter at a single post. Just a few years before Oberholtzer arrived, the HBC deemed the site important enough to warrant a new post being built in 1907. Although there were no more than six families actually living in town, it remained the hub of the fur trade for the shield country stretching off to the north, and it grew quickly. At the time of incorporation as a town in 1912, when Oberholtzer arrived, there were about five hundred people, and a census one year later pegged the population at 1,509. The boom had truly begun.

"After the railroad reached The Pas, I held my fur sales there for many years, usually two sales every year," wrote Arthur Jan, an English homesteader and entrepreneur who arrived in Canada in 1903. "There was always enough fur to create competition. Buyers came in from Eastern Canada, from New York, and St. Louis, but principally from Winnipeg. Bidding was always keen and I used to get the highest prices according to the market."

A few years after Oberholtzer passed through The Pas, copper and zinc were discovered some eighty miles to the north, and another new branch of the railway was extended to Flin Flon to serve the new mine. The Pas was partially eclipsed by a new frontier town to the north, and its economic basis shifted from furs to minerals. Nonetheless, The Pas was the railway junction—one branch to Flin Flon and one to Churchill—so it remained a vital distribution point for some decades to follow.

When another American canoeist, P. G. Downes, passed through here in 1939, he noted that times had changed for this erstwhile frontier town. "The Pas basks indifferently in departed glory," he wrote.

It was once the center of a booming optimistic mining fever, the jumping-off place for the North, the trapper's haven, the prospector's delight, scene of fabulous fur prices, dog races, high-stake poker games. Its citizens might awake in the morning to news of a 'strike' overnight or a man shot dead in a tree or kicked to death in a public latrine, or that a new fur buyer had bought a white cat skin for an Arctic fox. But these heroic days exist now only in the garrulous reminisces of the bar flies. For the frontier moved on; enterprise, money, enthusiasm, youth went seventy miles north to the thriving, jostling, polyglot mining town of Flin Flon.

Today, The Pas boasts a population of about six thousand. It remains a frontier of sorts, sitting on the banks of the still mighty, though muddy, Saskatchewan River, between the dense boreal forest of the rolling country to the north and the flat, fertile farmland to the south. The town's economy depends on serving the needs of these two diverse hinterlands—it still enjoys the same natural advantages, by dint of its location. The Opaskwayak Cree Nation, formerly known as The Pas Indian Band, which signed Treaty Number 5 with the Crown in 1876, registering 599 persons then, today numbers nearly five thousand, more than half of whom live on the adjacent reserve rather than in the town. They are nonetheless a vibrant force in The Pas and a major player in the local economy, an economy—based on furs, forestry, mining, and location as a transportation hub—that in many ways is the same as it was when Ernest Oberholtzer and Billy Magee took their Chestnut canoe off the train and carried it down to the riverbank to set forth on their grand adventure.

▷ ▷ *June 29. I got up at six and took a shave. At half past seven we began to canoe, using the tent as a sail. Soon we met a scow-raft coming down the river. Five white men had stopped to cook their breakfast. They were on their way to Le Pas, traveling day and night. Fine farm land on both sides of the river but timbered. Billy points out some black sand, which he says indicates gold. Our sail had to be lowered constantly but it helped us many miles.*

Three days into their "wilderness" trip, Oberholtzer and Magee were paddling on one of the busiest waterways in Canada. Scows, lighters,* steamboats, and canoes all made frequent passages up and down the river at this time. But for the impediment of Grand Rapids at the river mouth, where the Saskatchewan flows into Lake Winnipeg, the river was navigable with varying degrees of ease or difficulty all the way upstream to Edmonton. There were rapids, to be sure, and more than one of the larger boats failed to negotiate the boulder-strewn white water unscathed. Bill McKenzie, who worked on the steamboats from age fourteen in 1915 until the last steamboat run of 1924, remembered the challenging rapids where the "water was ripping all over and I wanted to see the ship miss those big rocks by inches. Those pilots had to know their business. If you ever stopped or missed the channel when you hit the boiling water, the boat would roll over like a ball." As a boy McKenzie watched the sternwheelers coming and going along the river and dreamed of the day he'd be old enough to sign on. As an old man in Cumberland House half a century later, folks still referred to him as "Steamboat Bill," such was his passion for the old sternwheelers.

The Hudson's Bay Company's 150-foot ss *Northcote* was the first of the large steamers to ascend the river, in 1874, making a journey of nearly five hundred miles upstream from Grand Rapids. The HBC saw it as a solution to their supply problem for the expanding trade to the northwest in the Saskatchewan and Athabasca districts. The press afterwards reported that "the steamboat just launched on the Saskatchewan is the forerunner of a great fleet of steam craft which is hereafter to navigate this long line of waterways," anticipating a connection through Lake Winnipeg, and the Red River down to the northern United States and perhaps even a connection to the upper Mississippi. Nothing like that would ever be achieved, of course, but nevertheless, these

---

* A lighter is a small boat, usually flat bottomed, normally used for loading and unloading ships at anchor in a harbor or for transporting goods in sheltered waters.

boats did carry passengers, in considerable comfort, as well as freight and ore, serving the growing frontier for fifty years.

Even the Mounties used the steamboats. Just days before Oberholtzer paddled here, Inspector L. H. French of the RNWMP had completed an inspection trip. "On the 11th inst I left [from The Pas] on the Steamer Brisbin & patrolled west to Joels tie camp, there are 30 men working in the camp at present, making ties for the H.B. Ry. & by the end of July Mr. Joel expects to have 75 or 100 men at work, there were no complaints," he reported.

Long before the *Northcote* and Steamboat Bill, the river was used by the Opaskwayak Cree, who in turn showed the white man the way to access the unknown lands to the northwest. First among the new arrivals was La Vérendrye who, in the mid-1700s, pushed the French fur trade and exploration up the Saskatchewan River. By the 1750s, the French operated a network of trading posts extending from Montreal across the country as far west as this very stretch of the Saskatchewan River. The difficulty and expense of transporting trade goods from Montreal and furs back, as well as the sheer distance to be traveled in a single season, effectively prevented the French from extending trade any farther west. The English, though confined to their posts on the shores of Hudson Bay, nevertheless posed a challenge to the French. For the Cree the competition made their furs more valuable and provided alternative sources of European goods, especially firearms and metal products. At times, the long trip out to the Bay seemed worth it.

La Vérendrye, trying to convince the Cree to maintain their trade exclusively with the French, spoke to their leaders, probably somewhere along the banks of this very stretch of the Saskatchewan River. As he recorded:

When you deal with [the English] you have to do it as if you were their enemies; they give you no credit; they do not allow you inside their fort; you cannot choose the merchandise you want, but are obliged to take what they give you through a window good or bad; they reject some of your skins, which become a dead loss to you after you have had great trouble in carrying them to their post. It is true that our traders sell some things a little dearer, but they take all you have, they reject nothing, you run no risk, and you have not the trouble of carrying your stuff a long distance.

In the face of such competition, the Hudson's Bay Company began to contemplate a move inland, despite a deeply rooted fear of the forbidding interior landscape and its Indians. Serving at York Factory at the time was a young man from the Isle of Wight, Anthony Henday, who had been convicted of smuggling in England and sent to the Bay as punishment. He volunteered to undertake the journey inland with the group of Indians gathered at York Factory for the trade when they set off for their home country in the spring of 1754. The Cree headman was Attickasish, who, in Henday's words, "has charge of me" and who duly assigned to his charge a young Cree woman as cook and interpreter, to whom the young Englishman referred in his personal journal as "my bedfellow." A month later in late July, they stopped at the French trading post at Pasquia on the banks of the Saskatchewan River, which his Indians called Waskesaw (Red Deer). Henday later wrote:

> We came to the french factory on my arrival, two french men came out, when followed a great deal of Bowing and Scraping between us, and then we Entered their fort, (or more properly a Hogstye) for in Short it is no Better, they have neither victuals nor drink. Except a little Ruhigan, they are very Lazey, not one stick of wood anigh their house; they asked me where the Letter was, I told them I had no Letter, nor did not see any Reason for one, but that the Country belonged to us as much as them; he made answer it did not, and that he would detain me there, and send me home to france, I told him I knew france as well as he did, and was not afraid to go their more than himself, which Made Monsieur a Little Cooler.

The French master and most of the men were away, taking furs down to Montreal, so in reality the post did not have the manpower to make good on the threats to Henday's party.

They did not detain him, but rather the two exchanged gifts of tobacco and pemmican, and two days later Henday left the post heading farther upstream. He spent that winter with the Indians farther west, noting the Blackfoot's use of horses on the plains and watching the buffalo hunt, both unprecedented observations. Ever a loyal servant to the Company, Henday attempted to persuade all the Indians to make the long journey to York Factory with their winter's furs, once the spring arrived. In some measure, he was successful, returning to his post on the shores of Hudson Bay on June 20, 1755, just shy of one year after his departure, accompanied by a brigade of sixty Indian canoes loaded with furs. Perhaps his immediate superiors did not want to hear his report of a fur-rich country with hospitable Indians. Henday was vilified and ridiculed for suggesting that Indians rode horses—his report was discredited. In this way, the less venturesome chief factors at Hudson Bay avoided any suggestion they should establish an interior trade, at least for the time being. It was easier to sit in the comfort of York Factory and let the Indians transport the furs to them.

After the fall of Quebec in the conquest of 1759, British "Pedlars" from Montreal assumed loose control of the French network of posts. Many of *les voyageurs Canadiens* continued to provide the knowledge and manpower needed for the great canoe brigades to cross the country every year. The Montreal-based fur trade enjoyed a resurgence. In some cases the newly allied Scottish and Canadiens traders intercepted Indian canoes along the Saskatchewan, headed for the Bay with a load of furs, with an offer to save them the trip. The approximate going rate was twenty beaver pelts for a gun, ten for a stroud blanket, and three for a one-pound axe. In 1768, the piles of beaver finding their way to Hudson Bay, and hence the London market, got smaller by half, compared with the average of previous years. By 1773, the take was halved again, with the return at York Factory that year down to eight thousand beaver skins. The HBC's profits shrunk. Something had to be done.

Veteran traveler Samuel Hearne, only just refreshed from his laborious walk across the barrenlands, had so impressed the Company's officers in London that he was assigned the task of forging inland from York Factory to the heart of Cree country and the Saskatchewan River "to establish a fort at Pasquia." Instead, he did better, in 1774 setting up a trading post farther upstream at Cumberland House, where the Indians could be intercepted before getting to the old French post at Pasquia, The Pas. Over the next fifteen years, the HBC established five more trading posts farther up the Saskatchewan River. Traders who volunteered for service at the new inland posts were given a special bonus. The HBC had fundamentally changed its approach.

In one of his private notebooks, some years before he set eyes on the place, Oberholtzer had recorded a solitary fact after reading Hearne: "Cumberland House was the first inland settlement the Company made from Hudson's Fort." Something in that fact had stirred him, adding fuel to the internal fire propelling him to see these faraway places.

In response to the HBC's move inland, the loose alliance of Montreal's Scottish merchants, New England adventurers, and French Canadian voyageurs formed the North West Company in the early 1780s. The new company sent as many as ninety canoes, each with eight or ten men, into the country west of Lake Superior and sold up to 200,000 beaver pelts in Montreal at year's end. The famous explorer Alexander Mackenzie wrote about this seesaw of prosperity between the two companies:

> The traders from Canada succeeded for several years in getting the largest proportion of their [Cree] furs, till the year 1793, when the servants of that [Hudson's Bay] Company thought proper to send people amongst them, (and why they did not do it before is best known to themselves), for the purpose of trade, and securing their credits, which the Indians were apt to forget. From the short distance they had come, and the quantity of goods they supplied, the trade has, in great measure, reverted to them, as the merchants from Canada could not meet them upon equal terms.

The battle for control of the western fur trade raged on, a nasty battle that involved booze, bribery, and bloodshed, until finally a bright, young businessman in London, John Henry Pelly, managed, on behalf of the HBC, to negotiate a truce and then, in 1821, a merger of the two rival companies. Peace thereby returned to the banks of the Saskatchewan River and its hinterland. As a direct result, Pelly was elected governor of the HBC, a position he held for thirty years, during which the company achieved its zenith of power and profits.

Meanwhile, the Hudson's Bay Company developed a new system of supply for the interior trade to replace the use of fragile birchbark canoes. York boats, which had been in use around James Bay for several years already, pushed inland up the Hayes River, across Lake Winnipeg, and on up the Saskatchewan River. The flat-bottomed boats, typically twenty-eight feet long, sometimes more, styled after an old Orkney design that in turn resembled a Viking longboat, crewed usually by six or eight oarsmen—sweeping twenty-foot oars—and a steersman, provided the backbone for the trade throughout the nineteenth century. The last York boat brigade arrived in York Factory in 1871, but there were still York boats on the Saskatchewan as Oberholtzer paddled upstream. At that point, they had been in steady use on the river for 115 years, since 1797. Inspector L. H. French of the RNWMP, in his June 1912 report, wrote further: "From here [Joels tie camp] I went on to Cumberland House, arriveing on the evening of June 12th, I visited the Settlers & Indians around the H.B. Post & I found every thing very peaceable & quiet. On the morning of the 13th I left Cumberland on the Steamer Brisbin, which had a towe of 6 York Boats for the H.B. Coy takeing them across Sturgeon Lake to Sturgeon River. These York Boats were on their way to Pelican Narrows, with winter supplies for the H.B. Co."

Though Oberholtzer does not mention any York boats on this stretch of the river—he did photograph some later in his trip—he must have been aware of their presence in general and almost certainly saw them on the river and at the docks in front of the trading posts. And one assumes that any traveler of his ilk would know something of the fur trade history that they reflect. This stretch of the Saskatchewan River was a central stage in the fur-borne drama that unfolded more than a century before Oberholtzer's passage. It was the nucleus of a phenomenon that defines a large part of Canada's history. On this riverbank both the French and then the English built their first trading posts in the west. And from these locations they launched their campaigns into the great northwest. To paddle on this stretch of the Saskatchewan River is to paddle into the heart of fur trade history.

On June 29, Oberholtzer and Magee brought their canoe up on the beach at Cumberland House, 138 years since it was established as a trading post by Samuel Hearne, whose descriptions of the barrenlands inspired their trip.

▷ ▷ *June 30. We got up at eleven o'clock as soon as the rain stops. An old Indian pays us a visit. Then Mr. Jones, a teacher and a clerk of the H.B. Co. came over and took me round to Mr. Cotter, the factor. I meet Mr. Belanger and we all discuss guides. Prices are very high on account of the railroad. Mrs. Cotter has me to tea. All men want $2.00 to $3.00 a day and pay for the return trip. I visit Edward Cadotte, a one-eyed half-breed in the evening. He can not go and I decide to go as far as Pelican Narrows alone. When I return to camp at ten o'clock (in the evening), I find Billy on duty and everything prepared for a bad storm.*

The storm ripped through the settlement that night, damaging canoes and downing wigwams and fences, by Oberholtzer's account. The next day, the cows got into the vegetable garden, and as he walked from his camp to the post to purchase some tea and bacon, he noticed the "dogs with sticks tied between their legs to prevent their chasing cows and children." At noon the Hudson's Bay factor served Oberholtzer a dinner of "delicious tender" moose meat, and by midafternoon he and Magee were ready to move on.

Cumberland House at that time was still, above all, a Hudson's Bay Company trading post, 138 years after its establishment by Samuel Hearne. The Anglican church had established a mission there in 1840, from which starting point most of the Native people in the surrounding territory were recruited to their church. For many years it was the hub of the fur trade in western Canada. Toward the end of the century, as other transportation routes opened and economic interests diversified, Cumberland House slowly declined. Nonetheless, it remains today the oldest, continuously occupied settlement in Saskatchewan. Cumberland House's significance to Oberholtzer reflects its very significance to history. It is here that he, like others before him, left behind the great east-west water highway of the Saskatchewan River to strike north. Here then is the true beginning of his quest, following the old way north.

Oberholtzer is much taken by the next leg of their journey, and the beauty of the landscape, writing more in his journal than before about their travel and his observations. They leapfrog along the way with two canoes paddled by Cree and Métis* men working for the Revillon Frères, trading rivals of the HBC.

▷ ▷ *These men all have a way of paddling that is new to me. It consists of a very rhythmical forceful stroke with a pause in between during which the paddlers frequently change sides. The top hand lets go entirely, the lower one slips to the top; and the paddle is swung deftly across the gunwales.*

The route moved upriver, climbing into the higher country to the north of the Saskatchewan River, away from the prairies, and up onto the Canadian Shield. The men paddled hard, portaged around rapids, or waded when they must, and they poled their

---

* The word "Métis" originated in the Red River valley, most often referring to the descendants of French Canadian fur traders and indigenous women, but in Canada it now refers more generally to people of mixed Native and European blood.

way upriver, a technique not easily adopted by the uninitiated. As they pushed upstream, an "HBC canoe with three half-breeds coming downstream" whisked by. Finally, after ten days' struggle, they reached Pelican Lake.

▷ ▷ *July 11. Just as we are camping for the night several canoes appear. One of them contains an elderly man, Mr. Christie, Manager at Pelican Narrows, an intelligent looking squaw, two well dressed halfbreed canoemen and a young man named Hall. He said his brother, who was passing in the canoe with a sail out in the middle of the lake, was just returning from a stay of four years at Ennadai Lake and that he would take the steamer at the end of July for Chesterfield Inlet. It had taken him 26 days to come down as far as Pelican Narrows; the route was bad, and there were no men to be had. When this young man had done all he could to dissuade me from attempting the trip to Chesterfield, he paddled on.*

This was Oberholtzer's first direct contact with a man offering personal insight into the territory that lay ahead, perhaps the first time someone had planted a seed of doubt in his mind about the intended route. Of Herbert Hall and his northern trading, more later; for now Oberholtzer's thoughts lay with getting to Pelican Narrows, just up the lake, and there hiring a guide. In camp that evening, the two men were taken by surprise when a York boat rapidly approached under oars, heading south, and landed just beside them. The York boat crew spent the night, much of it gambling and singing it seems, and were up and away early the next morning, even before Oberholtzer and Magee.

▷ ▷ *When I came out, I found the York boatmen straggling down to the boat with their personal packs, usually flour sacks. Some were washing their faces. The cook hastily distributed tea and the bannocks which he had been cooking all night, and then carried his whole kitchen (pantry) off in a box to the boat. The squaw took her seat in the stern, the steersman manned his oar, two men shoved with poles, a third on shore put his shoulder to the prow and crawled aboard just as the boat moved off. A man at each oar and one over, for this boat had two extra crews returning to Cumberland House. The usual crew consists of eight oarsmen, a steersman, a bowman, a guide, and lately (to save waste) a cook. As the boat moved out upon the calm lake, her great oars washing like the slow beat of a funeral drum, she was magnificent.*

All the activity along the way—Revillon Frères canoes, an HBC canoe, York boats, other unidentified canoes sighted across the broader lakes, an independent trapper from the country to the north, well-worn portage trails, and Cree camps—had to make it clear to Oberholtzer that he was following an old route, even if he had not already known, as he probably did. Canoes and York boats still plied these waters for trade, as they had done for more than a century. That era was, however, approaching its end.

▷ ▷ *July 12. At eight o'clock we started up the lake and, after a little uncertainty, found the narrow bit of a river, which connects the two parts of Pelican Lake. Several Indians were camped in the narrows and, just beyond, the real village appeared.*

On arrival in Pelican Narrows, Oberholtzer first spoke with the Revillon Frères trader, Mr. McLeod, and then paddled around the point on to the village center, where he walked "through wigwams and log shacks and innumerable dogs to the H.B. store where [he] met Mr. Thwaites and a halfbreed named Ely." The two great fur trade rivals of the time each used Pelican Narrows as their base of operations for all points north and west. Summer months saw almost daily arrivals or departures of canoe flotillas and York boats. The HBC post journal for 1912, during a six-week period that summer, records fifteen York boats arriving, ten York boats departing, nine freight canoes arriving, and seven leaving. That represents the movement of as much as 216,000 pounds of supplies and furs, supplies that had to be sorted, put in stock, or redirected northward and furs that had to be graded and bundled for shipping south.

The men who manned these boats and hauled this weighty freight were local Cree and Métis. The basic pay was two dollars per day, with extra for those promoted to bowman, steersman, or guide, up to as much as two and a half dollars per day. That top daily wage could buy twenty pounds of flour or five pounds of bacon at the post. A shovel cost a week's wages. These same men spent their winters trapping. The HBC account book of the time lists about eighty men so occupied. By comparison with the summer wages, winter was a time of plenty: five dollars for a beaver, six to eight dollars for a fox, seven to ten dollars for a marten, and fifteen dollars for a lynx or an otter, this latter price the equivalent of a week's wages for a York boat bowman.*

Though this post was in its heyday at the time of Oberholtzer's visit, there had been a fur trade presence on Pelican Lake since the late 1700s. The first HBC post was established briefly in 1818, and the contemporary post built in 1874. By 1912, the transshipment of goods and furs through the Pelican Narrows post had reached an almost unmanageable volume, particularly given the difficulty of ascending the river into Pelican Lake. A solution was developed the next year, 1913, with the institution of "horse-swings" to carry goods from The Pas. An old HBC man from the 1920s, Sydney Keighley, described a typical horse-swing.

> A swing consisted of five teams of four horses, each hauling two sleighs of freight. Each team hauled around ten tons or more. Because there were no paper or cardboard cartons in those days, protective packaging accounted for much of the weight. All goods were packed in wooden cases reinforced with metal strapping to withstand the rough travel conditions. A case containing fifty pounds of lard weighed sixty-five pounds. Flour was all double bagged with an outside bag of heavy cotton and there was little breakage or damage to goods during shipping. . . .

* All dollar amounts are in Canadian dollars.

Most swings were led by a team of two horses pulling a snowplough. The snowplough was attached to the front of a small platform with runners, where the lead driver stood. Occasionally the snowplough was fixed to the end of a push pole and it was pushed by the lead four-horse team, reducing the total number of horses in a swing from twenty-four to twenty-two. Bringing up the rear was a covered two-horse sleigh used for cooking and sleeping.

For the most part their route crossed frozen lakes and followed summer portage trails. A good day's travel was fifteen miles. The journey from The Pas to Pelican Narrows took from ten to twelve days; even so it moved more goods more quickly and with less effort than the old summer route by water. In addition to the freight goods, the horses had to pull their own feed, of course, bales of hay and oats perched atop each sleigh. Along the way, stables were built to shelter the horses from cold winter nights. "The stables were unattended and, like trappers' cabins, had neither locks nor caretakers. Travelers were welcome to use them for stopping places in case of need. Many times when tripping by dog-team, I overnighted in one of these stables—a most warm and comfortable place to be, tucked in amongst all that hay, with the temperature forty or fifty degrees below zero and often a nasty wind blowing outside," remembered Keighley.

By 1918, there were more than three hundred teams of horses working in the district from The Pas to Pelican Narrows, some of them engaged in hauling ore from the new mine at Flin Flon, some hauling fish down from the North, and others serving the trading posts at Pelican Narrows and beyond. Shortly after World War I, airplanes arrived, and within a few years it became practical to simply fly some goods into the far-flung trading posts, landing with floats (pontoons) on water in the summer and with skis on the ice in winter. With this development the need for horse-swings went into decline. Then transport trucks took over the heavy winter hauling, following ice-roads along much the same routes used by the horses. By the onset of World War II, the era of the horse-swing was coming to a close.

For hundreds, perhaps thousands, of years before all of this activity introduced by the white man, this country was essentially Cree territory, people who managed a subsistence life based on the food available from the land. The location of Pelican Narrows, in Cree, is Opawikoscikcan (The Narrows of Fear), at the heart of the traditional territory of the Assin'skowitiniwak (People of the Rocky Area), referring to the rocky country of the Precambrian Shield stretching across this part of the North in modern-day Manitoba and Saskatchewan. Opawikoscikcan got its name from an event that occurred long before the white man came to this country in significant numbers. A large group of Crees, occupying thirty tents, were once camped here for the summer, presumably attracted by good fishing at the narrows. All of the fit and able men in the group left with the winter's accumulation of furs, bound for a trading post to the east, probably all the way to the shores of Hudson Bay—such a long and difficult journey that the women and children were left behind in camp. While the men were away, some strange Indians from the south attacked the Cree camp and massacred all the women and all but two of the children, who were left to fend for themselves on a tiny island just offshore from the present-day village. When the Cree men returned shortly thereafter, they found bodies floating along the shore of the "narrows of fear." It is said that as recently as the middle of the last century, human bones were still occasionally washed out by the rains at Pelican Narrows.

A letter written in 1903 by the Indian Commissioner in Winnipeg describes the official view of Pelican Narrows: "These Indians are very closely associated with those of Cumberland [House] and the freighting of supplies and shipping of fur to and from points further north via Cumberland facilitates communication between them." Today the people are formally acknowledged as the Peter Ballantyne Cree Nation, named after the first chief, who had ceded a vast region of some eleven thousand square miles—his personal trapping ground—to the Crown in

1894 and later led the Cree of Pelican Narrows to their own treaty in 1900. He was still the chief when Oberholtzer arrived in 1912 and would remain in that role for another five years. The band then comprised a few hundred people. Today, including its mem-bership in other Saskatchewan communities, it numbers more than six thousand.

In the Hudson's Bay Company post journal for Pelican Narrows, the entry for July 12, 1912, reads: "Eli McDonald's and Jacob Ballendine's boats left for Beaver Lake warehouse about 4 P.M. Mr —— arrived from D3 [District 3, Cumberland House] who is on his way to Chesterfield Inlet." Whoever wrote this, probably Mr. Thwaites, must have been so busy, and have found Oberholtzer's name so strange, that he left it out, hoping to fill in the blank later, but never did. Besides dealing with fur and freight, the traders had gardens to tend, chickens and cows to husband, buildings to build and repair, and therefore lumber to cut, as well as firewood to cut, dog teams to feed, account books and journals to maintain, inventory to count, and no shortage of daily chores. On top of that, with all the comings and goings of post life, visitors were not uncommon. Most visitors arrived with a sense of purpose, in the employ of the government, the police, or the church. But here were two men traveling just to see the country, an objective that would have been little understood and probably even less admired. Nonetheless, Thwaites offered helpful suggestions in response to Oberholtzer's desire to hire a guide.

▷ ▷ *July 12. Besides Robey Mackeller whom Mr. Macleod [of Revillon Frères] had mentioned, they could only suggest Joseph McCullon. They told me Mr. Christie had gone to Cumberland [Oberholtzer recorded meeting him the day before.] and that they were getting ready to send two York boats to Beaver Lake. Some of their best workers were boys of eighteen. All of them were in the store buying handkerchiefs, mouth harps, candies, and other delicacies. They seemed a very high spirited lot; and Thwaites said they were the best boatmen in the north.*

Since it threatened a thunder storm, I hurried back to the canoe, where I found Billy placidly asleep. We put the tent up in a hurry among the bushes and brought all the things ashore. Then, as it was only drizzling, I shaved and went back to see the Priest, Father Guillaux. He was just at dinner with a halfbreed boy, who spoke French and good English. I saw bannock and a large baked fish on the table. The father himself looked worn and hollow-chested. He had on his robe and crucifix and looked about as clean as the average priest in Indian communities. The Oblate fathers, he says, are great favorites for the Indian work. Father Guillaux thought Joseph a better man than Robey particularly as Robey had been sick. Accordingly, I went up to Joseph's house where his wife and a number of girls in a wigwam were making moccasins. Joseph came to me looking very sleepy and finally accompanied me to the priest. He explained that he could not go but that an Indian councillor named John Neenin, who lives at the south end of Deer Lake, might be hired. The priest agreed to help me as soon as Neenin should arrive in the afternoon. Then I went back to the H.B. Store and, as soon as Neenin arrived, Ely went over with me and explained. Neenin said he would think about it. Soon afterwards I took a picture of the two departing York boats. Then Thwaites and I went over to an island for a swim; and when we came back I meet Neenin at the priest's. He wanted to travel with his family to the south end of Reindeer Lake, then in my canoe to Du Brochet and back in a birch-bark canoe which I should buy. He also wanted $2.00 a day paid in advance and food for his family. He had not come to a decision when I returned to Thwaites' house for supper; and that night in the tent I decided to go alone in spite of everybody's warnings. Thwaites and I had supper of his own cooking, his cook, a boy named Etienne, being away.

▷ ▷ *July 13. Raining a little in the morning, when I got up. I went around at once to the priest's where Neenin and several other Indians were going through some ceremony. I told the priest I did*

not want Neenin. Thwaites had told me one of his own canoes with
Solomon Cook as guide was to leave at noon.

Many years later, in 1939, the American adventurer P. G.
Downes flew into Pelican Narrows to begin a northern canoe trip
and recorded his impressions.

> Ascending a small hill, the path brings to view the full pano-
> rama and delightfulness of Pelican. The small, scrupulously
> white-washed trading post of the Hudson's Bay Company is
> set close to a sandy beach; the dwelling house, likewise white
> and with a red roof, lies farther back on a slight rise. From
> where I stood on a pleasant knoll topped with small birches,
> Pelican Lake, with its myriad low islands, stretched away to
> the west and lost itself in a great shining expanse to the south.

Much the same prospect lay ahead for Oberholtzer on his own
journey. He may well have climbed the same "pleasant knoll" to
take in the route before him prior to setting off. Whatever his
thinking, in reality he was embarking on the next leg without a
guide and leaving behind one of the more likely sources for such
a service. His opportunities ahead were limited, and he must have
known this, even as he "decided to go alone in spite of everybody's
warnings." But for now, he was comfortable to follow Solomon
Cook, however far that might help.

It did not help much. Within hours Oberholtzer and Magee
had lost sight of the HBC canoes and were left to make their own
way. Over the next three days, they "went up into a long bay and
wasted about three hours before [they] found the river" on one
occasion and, on another, lost "some time in the very crooked
channel leading to [Burntwood Lake]" but found their way "by
means of the tepee poles and cuts on the trees." They also had
some trouble finding Frog Portage over to the Churchill River.
Frog Portage, just three hundred yards long, crosses the divide between the Saskatchewan River and the Churchill River, a point of
great significance in the early history of Canada's Northwest. It is
the jumping off point for travel into the real Northwest, toward
Ile à la Crosse, Slave Lake, and the Mackenzie basin.

But that was not where Oberholtzer and Magee were headed; they wanted to go more directly north. Finally, after a week of difficult travel, on July 19 they reached Reindeer Lake and paddled up to the post at Southend where they once again caught up to Solomon Cook. He attempted to explain the route across Reindeer Lake to Billy Magee in Cree, which, though it is related to Ojibwe*—they are both in the Algonquin language family— was sufficiently different that Magee understood little. Early that evening, the two intrepid travelers headed out onto the lake, alone and uncertain but nonetheless determined to find their way to Lac du Brochet, some 160 miles to the north up Reindeer Lake.

⌄ ⌄ ⌄ ⌄ ⌄

That this was truly beyond the frontier, where Oberholtzer was now paddling, is perhaps most aptly illustrated by a contemporaneous report written by a Mountie upon completion of a winter patrol through this same country.

> On Feb the 8th I hired a guide at the rate of $3.00 a day + rations and left Cumberland House the same morning and arrived at Beaver Lake on the evening of the 8th and visited all the Indians the total number being about 20 and left on the morning of the 9th and arrived at Pelican Narrows on the afternoon of the 11th and camped at the Hudson Bay Post till the afternoon of the 13th and during my stay at Pelican Narrows I visited all the Indians. I also visited the RC Priest who stated the Indians had been very good during the year and were in good hunting grounds and making a good living. At Pelican Narrows there are about 25 families live, most of them being treaty Indians. I arrived at the South End of Reindeer Lake on Feb 17th, it taking me four and a half days from Pelican Narrows which is a distance of about 110 miles. During that four and half days travelling I was breaking trail through rocky portages and was very hard on the dogs. Having to carry dog feed from Pelican Narrows. I stayed at the south end of Reindeer Lake on Feb the 18th and gave the dogs a days rest. I vis-

---

* In Canada, "Ojibwe" is more commonly spelled "Ojibwa."

ited all the Half Breeds and Indians of the District, as they
were all at the south end of Reindeer Lake this day getting out
logs to build a RC Church. No of them had any complaint.
I then left the south end of Reindeer Lake on Feb the 19th for
Lac Du Brochet, which is about 160 [miles] up the north corner
of Reindeer Lake. While crossing I struck very poor trails and
used snowshoes most all the way and did not meet any body or
see any Indian camps till I reached Lac Du Brochet on the
afternoon of Feb 23. I camped at the Hudson Bay Co Post and
my guide went and camped with some half breeds who were
his relatives. I stayed at Lac Du Brochet till March the 5th and
during my stay at Brochet I visited all the people. The RC Priest
said the Indians were good living people around Brochet and
there was no cause for any complaint and he thought it was a
good thing for the police to make a trip up there once a year as
it keeps the Indians in good order. I left Brochet on March the
5th on my return trip...and arrived back at Cumberland
House on March the 15th. While crossing Reindeer Lake and
returning I seen large bands of reindeer. The total distance
from Cumberland to Lac Du Brochet and return is 700 miles
which took me 23½ days travelling at the average of 30 miles
per day. The dogs arrived back in Cumberland in good condition but thin. During the trip I received no complaints. Attached is copy of diary.
    [signed by B. Belcher, Corporal]

            ᴠ   ᴠ   ᴠ   ᴠ   ᴠ

The canoe route was not easy to find without a map. Reindeer
Lake is filled with thousands of islands, large and small. Though
they offer shelter for the paddler, they also serve to confound the
navigator. Fortunately for the pair, the weather cooperated, so the
paddling was not difficult, even in the long open-water stretches,
and they covered the miles quickly. Nevertheless, time and again
as they progressed northward, the men found themselves in a
dead-end bay, forced to retrace their steps. Four days after leaving
Southend, confident that the most northerly post lay just ahead,
Oberholtzer had a bath, "shaved, put on [his] green tie, and took

[his] pipe; all ready for du Brochet," but all in vain, for they did not find the post for another four days. Finally, during a breakfast stop on July 27, they "could discern four or five gleaming white patches on a hillside across the lake." It was the first sign in more than a week that the post at Lac du Brochet might be nearby.

▷ ▷ *Through my glasses I made out a number of tents and wigwams and the wisest course seemed to be to cross over for directions. We found an Indian encampment—the best one I have ever seen. One of the men—apparently the leader—could answer a few words in English.... The Indian leader, whose name turned out to be El Laurent, took me to the top of the hill to show me the fort, and, when I was ready to go, he got in his canoe and took us all the way across.*

Together with El Laurent, they paddled into Lac du Brochet, where the guide pointed out the HBC buildings. Oberholtzer paid El Laurent "half a dollar and some tobacco" for his trouble and went to meet the HBC factor, who "listened in astonishment to [his] plans." Clearly, Oberholtzer's first priority remained the search for a guide who would lead them up to, and across, the barrenlands. Within minutes he met Alphonse Chipewyan (more properly Alphonse Dzeylion) of whom he already knew. "Alphonse was the man that had taken Father Turquetil down to Churchill by dog team and returned in his canoe up the Little Seal. He looked like a good man." In the course of that first evening, Oberholtzer put a proposition to Alphonse, offered him "a salary of three skins ($1.00) a day," and left him to consider the idea. Alphonse's immediate reply was that he was not sure what to do with his wife and two children if he left on such a trip, wisely laying an escape route out should he decide he needs it. At the time a Dene man would have been disinclined to flatly refuse a white man's proposal, so this way, if necessary, he could blame his inability to accept on his family, with a hint of regret. It seems more

Alphonse Dzeylion, Lac du Brochet, July 28, 1912.
In Brochet in 2005, there was much discussion about the
identities of the three girls and the woman to Dzeylion's left.
Though it is not absolutely certain, the following consensus arose
(left to right): *Elyse Cook, born 1895, the daughter of Joseph Cook*
and Marie Linklater; Angelique Dzeylion, born 1905,
died in childhood; Eugenie Cook, born 1903, died 1922;
Eliza Cook (Philomene Umpherville's aunt).

likely, however, that he considered the payment offered to be insufficient, at less than half of what he could make working on a York boat where he would have less responsibility and less danger. Sure enough, two days later at the priest's house, Alphonse announced that he could not go "on account of his wife."

Oberholtzer's plan shifted gear as he now felt that "the only man left was Laurent," who in turn claimed that ill health prevented him from going. Oberholtzer faced a decision: With no guide was it sensible to go farther? His journal provides little evidence that he seriously considered the options, instead resorting to stubborn bravado.

▷ ▷ *I made up my mind that if he declined and declared the route to the Seal River impassable on account of the low water, I would start north with Billy either for Ennadai or for Churchill via Nueltin. Billy said he thought we could find our way. I was half a mind to go straight through to Chesterfield. At noon I met Laurent at the priest's and learned that the only way I could go east was by way of Nueltin; using preferably the northern (Nueltin River) river course.**

Lac du Brochet was a critical juncture in the expedition. Beyond this point the map became even more sketchy. With no more trading posts, the likelihood of encountering other white men was extremely small, and even Native travelers would have been few and far between.

---

* He is referring, presumably, to the river that reportedly flowed east out of Nueltin Lake known as the Thlewiaza.

3

At the Frontier

The twin-engine Navajo aircraft chartered to carry me and three others from the community of Wollaston Lake, Saskatchewan, to Brochet (formerly Lac du Brochet) in Manitoba—a half-hour flight from the northern reaches of one province into the northern reaches of the neighboring province—bounces along at just over one thousand feet in heavily overcast conditions, buffeted by the gusty spring winds. It is April 25, 2005. At this latitude snow is still on the ground, though the melt has begun, so the coniferous forests look black and the lakes are still covered in solid white ice. A gray day such as this offers up a black-and-white world of contrast. Looking down on the north country at this time of year, the old portage (now snowmobile) trails of packed-down snow from one lake to the next, through the woods, stand out clearly as sinuous white lines carving their way through the black spruce forest. This is well-traveled country in winter. The seemingly empty wilderness of lakes and trees stretching out beyond the horizon is in fact the hunting and trapping territory for the people of Brochet, who use trails no doubt worn down by their ancestors for eons.

From a plane one sees the country in a very different way than from a canoe. The sheer immensity of space, of lake and forest stretching off to the horizon in every direction, holds the eye as it cannot when on the surface. Yet one cannot appreciate the wildness of this country or the distances to be traveled—for that one needs to travel on the land or on the water under one's own power.

A minute before the pilot turns his aircraft for the final approach, I catch a glimpse of the town on the shore of Reindeer Lake, only a short distance to the southwest of the Cochrane River's mouth, a clue to the rationale no doubt underlying its location. From the air the town is a neatly arranged but irregular grid of dirt roads lined by small houses, with spur roads running out in various directions, one of them into the jack pine forest to the clearing that serves as our airfield. Inside the tiny terminal—a small shack badly in need of repair—there is just one employee, a young man with his hands full dealing with all the paperwork involved in receiving and dispatching the day's flight. Fortunately, another young man, who comes out to meet the plane in the vain hope of finding a part he has ordered for his snowmobile, offers some of us a ride in his pickup. While I struggle to stay atop my pack in the open back of the truck, we speed into town, bouncing and pitching along the rough road. The drive isn't long, but long enough for the cold air to bite at exposed skin, and both of us in the back duck down and face backwards to avoid the sting. Halfway into town, an occasional house begins to line the road, each one picturesquely set back from the road in its own small clearing and surrounded by a canopy of jack pine. Some have white picket fences. Others look less than well cared for. The trees end, and we emerge as if onto a field, now with a few dozen houses on either side of the road and in the center, a cemetery and an assortment of larger buildings that, it becomes clear, are the main features of Brochet's modern and historic infrastructure. The truck pulls up in front of St. Peter's Roman Catholic Mission.

In Brochet what could be more appropriate than first to be greeted by Sister Carmen, a stern nun who lives in the mission house across the street and runs the mission proper? She introduces the facilities, lays out the rules, many of which have to do with economy—don't use too much water, don't leave unnecessary lights switched on, always lock the door—and then bustles off across the way to her home. I feel somehow transported back in time.

˅   ˅   ˅   ˅   ˅

From the perspective of non-Native use, the site was first, but briefly, used by the Roman Catholic church at the outset of a convoluted series of events. In 1846, two Roman Catholic Oblate missionaries were traveling into the Northwest when they met some Dene at Frog Portage, the same crossing into the Churchill River used by Oberholtzer and many other travelers. The Dene had come south from Reindeer Lake to help with freighting goods up to Southend. The priests were headed northwest, upriver, on the Churchill, but they nonetheless paused to minister to the Dene, who were all Woods Chipewyan, already accustomed to such contact. The missionaries promised that one of them would travel to Reindeer Lake the next year. Fr. Alexander Taché was as good as his word, traveling several hundred miles by snowshoe to keep his promise. He was, by all accounts, a remarkable man, well liked by those he served. He had an open, round face, almost no neck, and the bulky body of a man who could endure hardship. During his wide-ranging travels to minister among the Indians, this young priest, who was just learning the various dialects of Cree and Chipewyan, preached through a translator. On one occasion he chose to instruct his listeners on the merits of chastity, *la chasteté*. The good Christian trapper duly translated: "Our Father, the Blackrobe, tells us we must hold the summer hunt *[la chasse d'été]* also, that hunting in the winter is not enough." Misunderstandings notwithstanding, Fr. Taché worked and traveled tirelessly. It was said by another priest at the time that "very few could keep pace with him on snowshoes, and he was perfectly at home in a canoe, even if the rapids were near and the daylight past."

When he met the Woods Chipewyan as promised, in March of 1847, he asked them to bring their northern relatives, the Caribou-Eater Chipewyan, with them for the next meeting the following year. The tireless priest may well have been surprised at how many of the northern Caribou-Eaters, the Idthen-eldeli, were waiting in the spring of 1848 when he returned once again to the south end of Reindeer Lake, for they had made a significant journey from their hunting ground to the north of the lake. These people relied almost exclusively on the caribou herds, whose migratory wanderings they followed, to provide them with food, fuel, clothing, and shelter. With such a nomadic existence, the Idthen-eldeli were a difficult target for both the missionary, who couldn't find them, and traders, of whom they had little need. But far-ranging travel was nothing to them, and there was evidently some interest in knowing more about Fr. Taché's brand of medicine. Fr. Taché called his efforts toward these people St. Pierre's Mission, though it would be some time before any actual mission infrastructure was built. After the success of 1848, Fr. Taché agreed that next year St. Pierre's Mission would meet at the north end of Reindeer Lake so as to be closer to the hunting ground of the Caribou-Eater Chipewyan. But circumstances conspired against him, and the missionary was unable to keep his promise this time. The Dene would not soon forget this betrayal.

Two more years went by before another missionary, Fr. Augustin Maisonneuve, ventured up to the north end of Reindeer Lake to pursue the theological objectives of St. Pierre's Mission. He found few Caribou-Eater Chipewyan in the area, the majority having given up on the church. Fr. Maisonneuve decided that it would be futile to establish a permanent mission at the north end of the lake. For the time being, at least, that put an end to Fr. Taché's vision.

〜 〜 〜 〜 〜

In 1859, an entirely unrelated circumstance altered the course of events in Reindeer Lake. The buffalo of the plains had been devastated by overhunting to meet the demands of traders seeking fresh meat, pemmican, and the highly prized buffalo robes used in every stylish carriage in Montreal, New York, London, and Paris. By way of example, one of the single biggest hunts in the history of Canada's West occurred earlier, in 1840, when a total of 1,630 Métis set out from the Hudson's Bay Company base at Red River, including more than 400 hunters and their families and at least 500 dogs. On the first day alone, these hunters killed 1,375 buffalo. One can only imagine the total number of buffalo killed that year by all the hunting parties taken together. It is little wonder then that by the mid-1850s the HBC was looking for an alternate source of meat to support the demand for pemmican, the essential fuel of the voyageurs' expanding efforts in the Northwest. Chief trader George Deschambault, in charge of the HBC's post at Ile à la Crosse in the Athabasca—north of the plains and previously highly dependent on buffalo pemmican—conceived the idea of using caribou instead. And who better to supply the meat than the Caribou-Eater Chipewyan? With this in mind, and probably aware of Fr. Taché's inroads among the people there, the clever Deschambault arranged for a group of Métis men to go to Reindeer Lake in the hope of meeting up with some Caribou-Eaters. Although previously not much attracted to the fur trade, they found appealing the idea of hunting extra caribou—which they did anyway virtually year round—and being paid in trade goods. And thus it was decided that the HBC would establish a post at Lac du Brochet in 1859.

It had long been the case that the HBC, being an English company, was more closely aligned with the Church of England's efforts to proselytise. Whether that played a role in this case, or whether the Caribou-Eaters' sore memory of the failed Catholic promise in 1849 was a major factor, is uncertain. What is known is that the Chipewyans invited the Anglican missionary Reverend Hunt, in northern Saskatchewan at the time, to establish a new mission at Lac du Brochet. Their chief, Catjedeyaze, undertook some religious instruction from the English missionary.

Not about to give up so easily, the Catholics sent a priest to the top of Reindeer Lake in the spring of 1860. The Dene, ever cagey and fiercely independent, hedged their bets and bided their time, to see which church best served their needs. Catjedeyaze struck a deal—he would become Catholic and send his youngest son to the priests for an education *if* they would get on with building a new mission. Fr. Vegreville did nothing on this visit but reported back to Fr. Taché that the population of Caribou-Eaters at the north end of Reindeer Lake filled as many as 130 lodges, housing 1,000 potential souls for his mission. Fr. Taché, now in charge of the district, could not resist such numbers, so Fr. Vegreville returned in December with instructions to build the long-anticipated St. Pierre's Mission to the Caribou-Eater Chipewyan. Fr. Taché sent two younger men to assist, Fr. Alphonse Gasté and Brother Perréard. Fr. Gasté would remain for many years, until 1901.

Now all three parties were satisfied. The Idthen-eldeli had the mission they wanted and a profitable arrangement with the new HBC post. The HBC had the source of meat it needed, and the establishment of the mission had managed to get all of the northern Chipewyan to abandon trade at Fort Prince of Wales, on the shores of Hudson Bay, and come instead to Lac du Brochet. The Catholics could count on the HBC to help provision the new mission and to attract a new flock into the church's sphere of influence. The uneasy alliance survived for many years, though not without its trials. All three were to some extent uneasy bedfellows. In 1867, Bishop Grandin visited St. Pierre's, was unimpressed, and declared that the mission should be closed—only Fr. Gasté's unwavering belief that Lac du Brochet would eventually become the main center of Catholic influence on all the peoples to the north, not only the Caribou-Eaters but also the Inuit, kept the fledgling community alive. In 1870, when the HBC did not fully resupply its post at Lac du Brochet and at the same time withdrew the traders, the Chipewyan took offence and eschewed the trade to the extent possible for some years to follow. In 1897, when the HBC threatened to close the post, Fr. Gasté immediately arranged for some free traders to take up the slack, with the full support of the church—the HBC promptly backed down and kept its post open, not wanting to lose any ground to the free traders. The early days at Lac du Brochet were not without some tensions. Nonetheless, the uneasy alliance survived and the tiny post on the frontier began to flourish.

On January 23, 1866, the HBC trader William Whiteway recorded in the *Post Journal* the arrival of four Chipewyan from the north.

*The Hudson's Bay Company post
at Lac du Brochet, Reindeer Lake, 1892.*

Two from Lac de Brousea [Lac Brochet] and two from Lac la Hache [Wollaston Lake]. They say that there is plenty of deer [caribou] at Lac de Brouchie [Lac Brochet] but no fur at all. The Indians wishes us to send for meat at their camps but it is a long way off. They were 7 nights coming in and our dogs is not at home so we are not able to send at this time but will employ them to make us some dryed provisions and send for it some other time. Pierre [Morin, an assistant] is trading the little they brought in and debting [giving credit to] them a little. Three Chipewyans arrive later in the evening—Red Head and two others. He is the Fort hunter, was 3 nights coming in from his camp and says the deer is scarce but they want us to send two sleds along with them.

A few days later, he added, "The Chip. are a hard set of miserly beggars to deal with but they will find themselves in the wrong box if they think to get their own way with me."

▽   ▽   ▽   ▽   ▽

In April of 1868, Fr. Gasté, accompanied by several Dene who knew the route, became the first white man to use the route north from Reindeer Lake to the barrenlands. His Caribou-Eater guides (called Montagnais by the Oblates) and their families had in the past met up with Inuit and seemed to look forward to the opportunity. They dragged sledges and walked through the slush of the spring thaw, until finally, beside the Kazan River in early June, they met some Inuit, for whom this must have been the first encounter with the Church. As Fr. Gasté described it, "All the strangers' attention seemed to be concentrated on me. Our Montagnais indeed tried to give them to understand who I was (by gestures as well as by words) but, despite all their efforts, the poor Eskimos were hard put, I imagine, to form a more or less accurate idea of my mission. It seems that my long black robe, its many buttons, as well as the crucifix in my cincture, puzzled them very much; they could not take their eyes off them." One

Father Alphonse Gasté,
1830–1919
(date unknown).

imagines they might also have been fascinated by Fr. Gasté's bushy beard and flowing locks. Though he was a large man, he had an impish, friendly face, which no doubt served to help bridge the divide between him and these strangers. After this short visit, the two groups dispersed in preparation for the hunt as caribou arrived from the south. Fr. Gasté's party then traveled west to Dubawnt Lake, known by the Chipewyan as Too-bwon-tué (spelled phonetically), meaning, roughly, The Lake with Water on the Edges. A very large, almost round lake, it has long been recognized as one of the last lakes in the barrenlands to become ice free in the summer, if indeed it does thaw, for often the center of the lake has not melted before freeze-up returns in the fall. This may explain why it was traditionally feared by both Dene and Inuit. Legends speak of huge monsters beneath the ice.

For eighteen days the Dene hunters were busy killing caribou, and their wives were busy drying meat beside Dubawnt Lake. In early July the Dene, now encumbered by a large store of meat, wished to renew their acquaintance with the Inuit. "It had been mentioned that we would form a single camp at the end of the hunting season, and I had been highly pleased at that decision. When the time came, a few of our Indians, in their haste to see the Eskimos again and to trade with them, prevailed upon the others to leave as quickly as possible and to spend with the Eskimos the time set aside to tarry on that particular spot. I had no objection to it." It was three days' march back to the banks of the Kazan River, farther downstream than before, where the Inuit had made their summer camp. Dene and Inuit celebrated together for the next twelve days. The priest tried to take advantage of the opportunity to encourage them to visit his mission and the trading post at Lac du Brochet. With this possibility in mind, five of the Inuit accompanied the Dene for the long trek south in order to learn the route. The party of about forty, including the five Inuit, reached the tiny settlement at Lac du Brochet on November 11. The seven-month journey was nearly too much for Fr. Gasté, who "almost died, hauled on a toboggan by dogs" back to St. Pierre's Mission. He survived and rejoiced when, two winters later, a larger group of Inuit arrived in Lac du Brochet for a visit, the first of many.

It was said among the Oblates themselves that the conversion to Roman Catholicism among the Caribou-Eater Chipewyan was assured on November 5, 1870, when Fr. Gasté said a Mass for his departed colleagues, former Oblates who had passed away. When the popular priest appeared before the Idthen-eldeli, unbeknown to him, his congregation saw a ghostly figure above and behind him, as if shrouded in smoke, the likeness of a man wearing an Oblate cross and a collar of white pearls. Later, when they explained the vision, Fr. Gasté noted to his surprise that their description could fit only his favorite teacher at seminary, a man still hale and healthy so far as the younger priest knew. Only three months later did the missionary learn that this same man, Fr. Mestre, his dear old mentor, had died suddenly some three months before. The vision had so impressed the assembled congregation that this news of its significance meant their dedication to the Roman Catholic faith was secure from that time on. It remains a vital parish today.

Life in the tiny settlement throughout this time is recorded for posterity in the sparsest of detail, principally in the journals of the HBC traders and in the *Codex historicus* kept daily by the Oblate priests at St. Pierre's Mission. But fortunately, one of the brothers assigned to assist Fr. Gasté kept a private journal.

ᵕ   ᵕ   ᵕ   ᵕ   ᵕ

Brother Celestin Guillet was born in 1842 in France. He came to Canada in 1868, departing from the French port of Brest on his own voyage of discovery in the same month that Fr. Gasté was setting off from Reindeer Lake to seek out new Inuit catechists in the country to the north. Br. Guillet's personal journal offers a rare glimpse into the early life at Lac du Brochet, where the Oblate brother arrived in August 1869. As Br. Guillet wrote: "At last I have arrived at the Mission, something I have long wished for. I know I will love it here. I will love the poverty and the isolation, bearing it willingly for God." He goes on to ask his God to be with him in his misery and expresses his thanks for being with Fr. Gasté. The "poor little church," he says, reminds him of the stable in Bethlehem, its altar covered in gray boards, its three little windows letting in only partial light. Br. Guillet soon went to work making preserves from the wild berries available in the surrounding country, raspberries and blueberries, and along with the other brother at the mission, he cleaned the house, cooked, cut firewood, did the laundry, fished and hunted for food, and prepared to open a classroom for the instruction of local Dene and Métis children.

On March 9, 1870, Monseigneur Grandin arrived by dog team from Ile à la Crosse for a prolonged visit to the frontier mission. It was clearly an occasion for joy and celebration. Among other things, his visit coincided with the first visit, just a few days later, by the Inuit whom Fr. Gasté had contacted nearly two years earlier during his trip to the barrenlands. Br. Guillet described the procession of the sacrament on June 12.

Today the large grounds of the Mission are changed by a beautiful road. Mr. Courris of the HBC has given over his store to the missionaries. His staff are dressed in bright colours and the native flowers and the trees are draped in red and white with ribbons of all colours, covering everything available. Alexis LeCrie carried a great white flag decorated with a red cross and was certainly very proud.

At 1 A.M. the Red Indians followed the procession in two lines and came to understand something of it despite their savagery. Mgr. Grandin led the procession to the arc de triomphe where it stopped. We sang a hymn and Mgr. said the benediction. The procession then marched back, singing a sacred song of the holy sacrament in Dene that the savages knew and loved. It was a superb effect under all the greenery of the spruce covering the top of a little hill that they climbed in stages.

Father Gasté said the sacrament from a box elegantly cut and covered with gold paper. The songs of the Mission were magnificent with the beautiful voice of Mgr. dominating. It was more beautiful here so far from civilization, so close to the Arctic Circle. In our little corner of earth, so close to Heaven, we also sang with enthusiasm the blessings of the sacred sacrament and the songs of the Dene.

Br. Guillet wrote regularly, to describe the comings and goings, the problems and the joys, in the tiny settlement. The winter of 1870 and 1871 brought "a long period of deprivation as the fishing failed" when "the children from time to time would eat a little meat and it was the same with us." The barges were late arriving the preceding summer, and for some reason that was the year the HBC did not fully resupply its post. Some people died of starvation. It was that November when the vision appeared before Fr. Gasté's congregation, and Br. Guillet duly recorded the fruits of this most memorable occasion, and subsequent events, in his ongoing journal.

Four or five Dene were baptized, after living in sin and inhabiting the world of the devil, encouraged by the loss of the drum and hand games, replaced by a new order. A caravan of thirty Eskimos arrived to trade.

In this month [now January 1872] two boys of Mr. Charles Thomas, Protestant like their father, married. Daniel with Sophie Linklater [daughter of the "English Métis" Peter Linklater] and fifteen days later Geordy (Georges) with Adelaide Morin [daughter of the HBC employee Pierre Morin, also Métis]. Both were first cousins and now also sisters-in-law. Naturally they were not married in the church. Pierre Morin, a fervent Christian [by which the Brother no doubt means Roman Catholic] and father of Adelaide, did not give his consent but he had no authority. All the people of the Mission were invited by M. Courris to the first-rate feast for the wedding of these children. The dinner was huge dishes of meat—what a meal! A very grand party as the night passed with festivities. The dogs also did their part. Finally the famous violin signalled the dance, the sound surpassed by no other. Those who had full stomachs could not exercise too much. But thanks be to God there was no disorder, the dance among the Métis and the Indians was not as perilous as among the civilized youth of Europe.

Alternately this winter [1871–1872] there was a little hunting. The caribou were always several days march. At last the savages arrived, a few from all directions, carrying a little dried caribou for smoking. In spring they will finish the drying in the sun. These were our provisions for summer because at the Mission we do not fish in the summer as the fish are very rare at this time. The fishing commences only with the return of the barges at the end of August, and with the engagement of two Indians to catch fish to nourish us and their families. Several times they not only kept the fish for themselves but also reclaimed the dry meat of poor Father Gasté. It was too much but I had no power over this.

Babies were baptized, sinners were converted to the Roman Catholic faith, and the missionaries' sphere of influence continued to expand. On occasion one or another of them would leave the mission for a round of visits to the Dene camps to the north. Br. Guillet considered the possibility of traveling all the way to the barrenlands to visit the Inuit camps but was restrained by a concern that "a residence with them would be an impossible project, too difficult for missionaries." On one occasion, during the winter of 1874 to 1875, Br. Guillet offered a vivid description of his own travel for Christmas among the Dene.

Night was arriving and it was late. By 8 or 9 I could not see the trail and I stopped. I saw to the right a great expanse before me and I hoped to see by the light of the moon. I did not find the camp so I bedded down on spruce branches with my dogs but I did not sleep well because I was watching the team. I covered myself in caribou fur but was without a fire. I could not find a bit of dry wood in the middle of the spruce, so I waited for the rising moon.

By 5 o'clock in the morning I had not slept because of the cold. The sky was clear but still I could not find the trail so I headed out onto the lake to look. It was a quarter moon. I found the trail when I made a large crossing and the dogs knew it well. Their ears perked up and they saw in the direction of a small island some distance away that there were caribou. We left the trail, the team going with such great speed that I could not hold them. . . . The dogteam was some distance and I did not have the line and they were too far to reach, labouring in the snow. I hoped I had not lost my dogs. I did not have the strength to advance in the snow. I had no snowshoes and was alone. The caribou had gone and the dogs were chasing them. At last the caribou came back onto the lake and after them the dogs. I looked for the toboggan in the bush as the dogs had broken their traces in the woods and the toboggan had stopped very far into the bush. Finally I caught my dogs.

They were tired after going so far. Their tongues were hanging out and they wanted to sleep in the snow. I forgot my fatigue in sorting all of this out and I took precautions so my dogs would not go on another adventure. I put two lines on the toboggan with the dogs in a row and tried to make a small fire, but had no dry matches. I had to find the trail. I had nothing to eat. Good God! I knew I was very cold but I would not leave my team to get warm by walking. One time I was sure I had found the portage but there was no Indian camp as I had remembered, but again a lake, and for a third time I made camp with my dogs. After a long time I came upon a large lodge (in the camp the Indians put two lodges together and use this for prayer and singing when they gather on Sundays and for obligatory Feasts). I was going to unharness the dogs but was stopped by the hand of an old Indian woman who said, "Your hands are frozen, in fact your fingers are white." She rubbed them with snow which is the best remedy and God gave me strength and my circulation returned. After a little while all the Indians gathered and the singing of the carols of Christmas began. It was a beautiful sound in the middle of the woods. It is the birth day of the Divine Infant. I told the story in the little chapel, said prayers and several words about the songs and Pater Ave for St. Peter and for our diocese and our missionaries. We ended with a song, Eku sora soummarin nou'niniye koutte si, "thank you our Father, we are happy and content."

Now we made a feast and I was very much in need of food. I said the Benediction and all the men of about 25 or 30 were served first. Next the young men and little boys, third the women, the old people and the little girls and, at the back, the poor little orphans. Only the men ate together. This was the case among all the Indians. For the orphans, they stayed back and cleaned up what was left before it was thrown to the dogs. While the feast continued the men smoked their pipe, using the same one, a large black pipe, very well-made and well-used.

After noon we recited the prayers with the children and did a bit of catechism and again in the evening all gathered to sing in the big lodge for chapel and carols. It was cold but very nice in the lodge as it had been well-vented and made with strong wood. I slept well into the afternoon. The Indians were in charge of my team and I hired a young man for the return journey. I arrived at the Mission after a lively journey.

It is a measure of the Catholic missionaries' success among these people that the following Easter, in 1875, Br. Guillet estimated between 350 and 400 Dene gathered at the mission for the celebration. That summer Mgr. Grandin came to visit St. Pierre's again, this time coincident with the confirmation of eighteen new Dene candidates. His coming, as always, was a grand event; in anticipation of his arrival, Fr. Gasté announced: "I am going to wash the windows in the gables of the chapel. From there I can see the lake. From there I can watch both the point and the large rocks. I can come when I hear the loud cries from the fort that Mgr. has arrived, and also the sound of the guns." He did not have long to wait. Only minutes later, the shots of celebration rang out. From a canoe in midlake came two *feux-de-joies* in response. Beside himself with joy, Fr. Gasté would not let himself believe it until he saw, from the church's belfry, the canoe approaching. Fairly shrieking with delight, the priest ran to the beach to greet his monseigneur. Mgr. Grandin stayed for a week, a time of celebration, with benedictions, processions, confirmations, first communions, absolutions, marriages, and, at the end of it all, a grand feast. The *Codex historicus* calls it "a year of grace and blessings."

In August, Br. Guillet and his colleague, Br. Labelle, went fishing for the mission supply.

> We spent the month of August finding a new spot but sadly could not find a place as good as last year. We tried along the length of the river on the suggestion of the Indians but with very little effect. It was flooded and it was necessary to stand in the water. It was a place of peat, all flooded and offered no resistance but rather we sank in. When we came back—a young Dene was with us as our guide—but he had not helped us a bit in our work but he still depended on us to eat. We did not have many provisions as we had hoped to arrive within a day, but the wind was blowing very strong and in the end when we arrived on the lake the rollers were enormous. When heavy waves were breaking over the bow of the canoe it was as if it would split—we realized the need to land to reattach things with ropes and rearrange things a little. But poor Brother Labelle was terrified and was sick to his stomach.
>
> It was 5:30 at night and we had not eaten since morning and then only a little. Also he was depressed and rested a little while, knowing however that it was necessary for us to go on. The wind lowered a little and it was after 10 o'clock when we arrived at the Mission, horribly fatigued and hungry.

Mercifully, that fall the mission put up four thousand fish for the winter ahead, mostly necessary to feed the dogs.

Before the decade was out, an event of great significance occurred at St. Pierre's Mission: the chief of the Caribou-Eater Chipewyan was baptized. He was known by the priests as Tête Rouge and is remembered, even today, as Redhead. His proper name was Etienne Alphonse Betshi Delkozi. His conversion was important because, as the *Codex historicus* records, "By virtue of his uncontested authority, it was he who decided the conversion of all the tribe. Soon 50 adults were following to baptism." A few years later, he married. Notably, the *Codex historicus* records the marriage, on July 4, 1891, naming his father as Eyune (Strange One), and his mother as Banlayslini (White Man Devil). These clues, in addition to his nickname, all suggest that he was of mixed blood, a Métis, though clearly his own community looked up to him and accepted him not only as one of them but as their leader. His baptism was likely the high point of Fr. Gasté's many years at Lac du Brochet, without argument the most significant single conversion he achieved.

Redhead was a wise and powerful man, even though this was before the signing of any treaty with government, which event (some years later, in 1907) led to the formalization of the election of a chief for the band. Before that, though less formal, the chief's power fell to him purely by dint of his nature and influence. When a Geological Survey of Canada team passed through Reindeer Lake in 1881, they were confronted by the chief, who claimed to speak for all 386 Chipewyan attached to Lac du Brochet. Redhead sought to inform the government that, before any plans to extend the railway—which he had heard about, in the south, if not seen—into his country were advanced, the Chipewyan wanted to be consulted and to reach an agreed treaty. He was ahead of his time.

Fr. Gasté and Br. Guillet both stayed on at St. Pierre's Mission until 1901, by which time ill health visited regularly upon both men, no doubt the result of all the hardship both had endured over the previous thirty or forty years of living at the frontier. The two had been there since the mission's early days, Fr. Gasté even

*The old Roman Catholic Mission, at Lac du Brochet in 1894,
with four men standing outside, including Fr. Gasté
(second from the left).*

before Br. Guillet, but both men had seen the outpost struggle through difficult times and had guided the mission through its nascent era. It was at St. Pierre's that both men reached the pinnacle of their life's work. Br. Guillet fell seriously ill in 1909 and died two years later in Edmonton; Fr. Gasté died in 1919 after a long illness at age eighty-nine. They are remembered as the two men who built St. Pierre's Mission into the force it was to remain long after their passing. It was they who realized Fr. Taché's vision for the frontier. Fr. Gasté, with Br. Guillet's help, nurtured the fledgling mission until it became the center of Catholic influence in the north, not only for the Caribou-Eaters but also for the Inuit. Lac du Brochet maintained this frontier role for many years after the two men were gone.

⬯   ⬯   ⬯   ⬯   ⬯

The man largely responsible for motivating Ernest Oberholtzer to follow the old way North, J. B. Tyrrell, also forged the only connection to the route's earliest white traveler, Fr. Gasté. In 1894, Tyrrell stopped at Lac du Brochet on his way north to the Kazan River. He must have spoken with the priest about the route, although the details of those conversations are lost.

Joseph Burr Tyrrell, when he arrived in the small outpost, would most certainly not have gone unnoticed. He was an imposing figure, six feet tall with wire-rimmed spectacles, fair hair, and a trim moustache, though probably bearded by this point in his long summer of canoe travel. His paddling journey began June 23 at the mouth of the Saskatchewan River when the party's two nineteen-foot Peterborough canoes were launched above Grand Rapids. They arrived in Lac du Brochet nearly four weeks later on July 18. "Up to the time of our arrival at this place we had travelled in canoes for 650 miles, through country which was already to some extent known, at least geographically, and we had therefore hurried forward towards the unknown country ahead of us, devoting all the time caused by necessary delays to an inspection of the adjoining rocks, and not to the making of any regular geographical survey."

In Lac du Brochet, Tyrrell engaged two local Dene men, Thebayazie and Casimir, to act as guides for the relatively unknown route lying ahead, traveling in their own canoe and assisting with the portages. The second (probably senior) guide, Casimir, would rise to prominence among the Chipewyan Caribou-Eaters in the years ahead. Nevertheless, Tyrrell was not impressed, describing him as a poor canoe man, apparently afraid of the water. Partway through the journey, Casimir abandoned the explorer and offered his nephew Savasis (also known as St. Pierre) in his place. All three of these men provided Tyrrell with a sketch map of the route ahead (see p.11), even though, as an elderly Dene man, Pierre Besskkaystare told me, "Dene didn't use a map, it's in here," pointing to his head. Tyrrell must surely have also used the opportunity at the last outpost of civilization to discuss the route with the friendly priest, Fr. Gasté, but he did not tarry. Two days later, the Tyrrell party once again launched their canoes and headed north into the relatively unknown and certainly unmapped country between Reindeer Lake and his objective, the Kazan River. The surveying work began in earnest,

As recorded by J. B. Tyrrell in 1894, these are
"our two Chippewyan Indians [Thebayzie and Xavierseese]
near Ennadai lake. From Kazan River. Aug. 10."

"measuring the quiet stretches with a Massey's floating boat-log, estimating the stretches of running water, taking the bearings with a prismatic compass, using a solar compass occasionally to correct the variation, and taking the latitude daily, if possible, with a Hadley's sextant of seven-inch radius, and a mercurial artificial horizon." It was this care and attention to detail that enabled Tyrrell to produce the first map of the route to the barrenlands, the same map that eighteen years later would be Oberholtzer's only guide.

A week later, the Tyrrell party had moved out of the thick forest and into more open esker country where the trees are confined to smaller groves. They were now, at last, going downstream, having crossed over a divide some 120 miles north of Reindeer Lake.

> The route descends the stream through Thanout and Theitaga lakes, by the former of which an Indian chief named Red Head has a small but substantial log house in which he spends the winter. From Theitaga lake the Thlewiaza (or Little Fish) river was said to flow north-eastward to Nou-el-tin, or "Island-lying" lake, beyond which it flows, at first down a series of heavy rapids, and then with quieter water, until it empties into the west coast of Hudson Bay between Egg Island and Cape Eskimo.

This little tidbit of information on the Thlewiaza would be as valuable to Oberholtzer as Tyrrell's map when it came time for his own journey in 1912.

Not long after passing Redhead's cabin, Tyrrell left the Thlewiaza watershed and crossed the divide to the northwest in order to gain the headwaters of the Kazan River. He made his first camp there, on the shores of Kasba Lake, on August 5. Ahead of him now lay the challenging descent of a major, albeit still unknown and unmapped, barrenlands river and encounters with the large population of inland Inuit. It was the descriptions of these experiences that, just a few years later, captured the imagination of a young Ernest Oberholtzer.

▿ ▿ ▿ ▿ ▿

The year before Fr. Gasté left Lac du Brochet, his replacement, Fr. Turquetil, arrived, another Oblate who was to become a veritable legend in the North. Not long after his arrival, he would follow in Fr. Gasté's footsteps and undertake the arduous journey north to the barrenlands in order to visit the Inuit. It was a life-altering experience for him. He set out from Reindeer Lake the day after Christmas 1901, not to return until Easter. In 1906, he made a similar trip, such was his determination to bring the Inuit into the Roman Catholic flock. On the first occasion, the travel was difficult in the extreme, in winter conditions with raging blizzards and temperatures reaching forty below, but Fr. Turquetil was young and fit. He carried no extra pounds on his lanky frame. At times during these trips, he knew hunger as he had never imagined possible; he himself called it famine. On one occasion in the barrenlands, having caught a fish through the ice, Fr. Turquetil claimed to have bitten into the live fish and then, ashamed, looked about to see if anyone was watching. Despite it all, as the *Codex historicus* records, "the father persevered to learn enough of the language to practice the ministry without constraint."

His second trip, in 1906, began on April 24 and lasted until November 18. He traveled to and fro across the vast landscape, finding the opportunity to enjoy the warmer months on the barrenlands. He spent the summer in an Inuit camp beside Ennadai Lake on the Kazan River. Though he no doubt perfected his ability to speak their language, he apparently remained intrigued, if not discomfited, by their lifestyle.

> How about boiling the meat? It may take four or five hours of cooking something a little less raw, but there is nothing to do about it. The fire is lit. The container is in place, that is outdoors on the ground, at the mercy of the dogs who have licked it clean, having been called for that purpose. The same is true of the great trencher of wood or stone which serves as the meat plate.
>
> Most of the time, the water used for cooking the food does not come from the lake. A small slough in the midst of the rotten mass of the swamp, yields some water, of a mysterious colour between black and green.

The inside of the lodge was obscure. Everyone is lying face down around the plate. In the bullion, enriched with leftovers from previous meals, two whitefish float, boiled as is, neither scaled nor emptied [gutted]. One of the guests carves, another pulls off, a third one grabs a piece, bites into it with vigor and throws it back into the plate. Silence. All the jaws are functioning. Suddenly the lips open, the teeth are clenched and a powerful stream of scales, bones, and mashed flesh issues from each mouth aimed at the plate. The bouillon rocks and leaps with the impacts. The thumb and other four fingers quickly follow into the plate, searching for the rest, large or small. Four heads delve into the bouillon which is soaked up in a wink.

Just as Fr. Gasté, thirty-eight years earlier, had written, "One has to know the asperities of the ground over which we were travelling to have an idea of how much I was called to endure," Fr. Turquetil, in his turn, blamed the exertions of his 1906 journey to "the Eskimo land" for two years of subsequent ill health.

In the summer of 1905, Fr. Turquetil was joined at St. Pierre's Mission by another young and energetic priest, Fr. Egenolf. Unlike his immediate superior, who was from the beginning drawn farther north, Fr. Egenolf became immersed in the language, culture, and well-being of the Chipewyan. He was to remain at Lac du Brochet for decades. Not so Fr. Turquetil. In 1910, he was sent farther north to establish the first mission to the Inuit at Chesterfield Inlet on the west coast of Hudson Bay. From that day on, the spirit of St. Pierre's Mission was embodied by Fr. Egenolf. He is remembered fondly today by the elderly of modern-day Brochet.

⌄   ⌄   ⌄   ⌄   ⌄

The early 1900s was an era of great significance for the indigenous peoples of this region. The influence of non-Native culture had reached a point where virtually no one was still entirely beyond its reach: Cree, Dene, or even Inuit. Lac du Brochet was something of a focal point for this phenomenon. Some Cree families, who had been drawn north by involvement in the shipping of goods north up Reindeer Lake to the frontier post, had settled permanently. Chipewyan increasingly allowed their attachment to the post to define their lives. Inuit came south for visits in ever-larger numbers, sometimes just for trade, sometimes in desperate flight from famine, and occasionally they remained to become part of the community. The HBC records from 1881 note that there were 217 Inuit who "belonged" to the post at Lac du Brochet, alongside 386 Chipewyan and 29 Cree. Those numbers all continued to grow, though belonging did not mean residing, in most cases. The trade at the HBC post averaged returns slightly more than seven thousand dollars a year through the 1880s and increased to fourteen thousand dollars in 1900, a measure of the growth in activity at Lac du Brochet.

The turn of the century brought the zenith of a shifting trend in land use patterns that had begun almost a century before. Through the nineteenth century, Inuit had been moving inland, up the rivers that flow into Hudson Bay and overland to the banks of the Kazan River, sometimes even farther to the south shore of Dubawnt Lake. Coincidentally, the Dene had moved south and west.

When Samuel Hearne crossed this country in 1770, he encountered no Inuit, only the Chipewyan Caribou-Eaters, the "Northern Indians," as he called them, in large camps extending to the north end of Dubawnt Lake. By the time Fr. Gasté made his remarkable journey in 1868, his Chipewyan companions viewed this same country as the "Eskimo land." Three major events occurred back in 1782 that began this shift in territorial use. The French captured and destroyed Fort Prince of Wales, so the Chipewyan looked for new places to trade at the posts newly opened in the Lake Athabasca district to the southwest. In the same year an epidemic of smallpox swept through the Dene camps, killing hundreds. By the 1890s, the Inuit had occupied nearly all of the southern barrenlands, encroaching even into the margins of the subarctic boreal forest. Dene territory, which had long included so much of the barrenlands, had now contracted to the south and west.

J. B. Tyrrell, when he descended the Kazan in 1894, estimated the Inuit population along its banks at roughly one thousand. Notably, his Chipewyan guides turned back from Ennadai Lake, just three days into paddling the river, out of fear of encountering Inuit in the land ahead. The total Inuit population of the southern barrenlands, comprising the watersheds of the Thelon and Kazan rivers, was probably about 1,400. Tyrrell described the camps along the Kazan as comprising a few families, with their caribou skin tents and their caribou meat laid out to dry in the sun. He wrote of Ahyout, Hikuatuak, Kakkuk, Unguluk, and Pasamut and offered a glimpse of life as it once was beside the Kazan River, describing "a place called by the Eskimos Palelluah," more properly Padlerjuaq, meaning roughly the Place with the Big Willows. Here, Tyrrell watched Inuit hunters in their kayaks spear caribou as they swam across the river. A century before, Hearne had encountered Chipewyan hunters at the same location, waiting to intercept the caribou they knew were approaching on their migratory march. It was here, at this "celebrated deer-crossing place," that Hearne crossed the Kazan River in 1770.

Whereas the Inuit positioned their camps at likely caribou crossings and waited, the Dene were more inclined to simply follow the caribou in their migration, not unlike a pack of wolves. The two peoples had this fundamental difference in their respective strategies for survival, though they both depended upon the caribou. Both groups well knew the pain of desperate hunger, but it could be fairly said that often the inland Inuit—relatively recent arrivals—were living more precariously balanced on the edge. For Dene and Inuit, this was very much the reality of their lives even at the turn of the twentieth century, in the vast hinterland that lay to the north and northwest of Lac du Brochet. One of the most extraordinary aspects of this tiny outpost at the frontier was the fact that both Dene and Inuit, in significant numbers, had for some years been making regular visits, as had Cree and Métis freighters from the south.

▽ ▽ ▽ ▽ ▽

To the Dene attached to Lac du Brochet, 1907 was a year of great significance. That summer a man by the name of Thomas A. Borthwick, commissioner for Treaty No. 10, along with his party, arrived in the country. Borthwick, acting on behalf of the federal Department of Indian Affairs, was there to sign a treaty with the people whose traditional territory the government now wished to develop. The treaty party, which included a doctor (the government had previously pledged to provide medical assistance), arrived at the north end of Reindeer Lake by canoe on August 17, 1907. He was ten days behind schedule, unavoidably detained by his summer's travel, and so the Dene were waiting. His arrival had been much anticipated ever since an exploratory meeting of the commissioner with some of the Dene at Lac du Brochet the previous summer. While waiting, they had been engaged by the Hudson's Bay Company and the newly established competition, Revillon Frères, and had been paid for their labors with provisions. The treaty commissioner wrote:

> On the morning of August 19 I held council with the combined Indians of the Barren Land and the Indians of Lac la Hache, the Rev. Father Turquetil acting as interpreter, which he did on all subsequent occasions during my transactions with the Indians here, the Chipewyan language being spoken. I explained to them why I was sent to meet them, and after various thoughtful questions put by the Indians bearing upon the treaty and answered by me to their satisfaction, they asked for a short recess to discuss the terms of the treaty more fully among themselves; which was granted them. At 2 p.m. they reassembled and the Barren Land band announced that they had elected their chief [Petit Casimir] and two headmen, and were prepared to accept the terms of the treaty. The Lac la Hache band intimated that some of their people were away, but would be back in a day or so, and that they would like to have their concurrence in the matter of selecting their chief and councillors; I consented to their waiting a day or so, if necessary, in order to obtain the full consent of their band to their transactions. The chief and headmen of the Barren

Land band then formally signed the treaty, and without further undue delay the payments of their gratuities and annuities were begun to them, and were got through with at noon on the 21st. The number of Indians treated with in this band was 232, including 1 chief ($32), 2 headmen at $22, 229 other Indians at $12.

The Lac la Hache band assembled on the 22nd, and after the terms of the treaty were read over to them for the second time and thoroughly explained in their own language, they presented their elected chief [Thomas Benaouni] and two headmen, who then in due form signed the treaty, and the members of the band were paid in accordance with the terms of the treaty. The number of Indians paid in this band was 97.

It was that simple. By August 24, after just a week at the outpost, Borthwick's work was done. He and his party loaded up their canoes and headed south, leaving behind 329 new signatories to Treaty No. 10. It should be noted that 329 was probably less than half of the eligible Dene, evidence perhaps that Borthwick had done less than a complete job. Casimir, the newly elected chief of the Barren Land Band, had received the assurance his people wanted, that their hunting, trapping, and fishing rights would be unaffected by this treaty. With that impediment discarded, they had willingly accepted the government's offer of a one-time twelve-dollar gratuity and a smaller future annuity. Their concerns were more prescient than anyone present, probably including Borthwick, realized. It seems evident now that, having just established the new provinces of Alberta and Saskatchewan and laid plans for their settlement and development, Ottawa wanted to extinguish the aboriginal title to the land in the region. Treaty seemed a gentlemanly way to accomplish this aim. But as Frank Oliver, the federal minister of the interior at the time, had said in the House of Commons the year before, on March 30, 1906, "If it becomes a question between the Indians and the whites, the interests of the whites will have to be provided for."

Every year, henceforth, these Dene would assemble at Lac du Brochet for treaty day. Casimir would don the navy blue captain's

jacket, with its brass buttons and regal air, that he'd been given by
the treaty commissioner. All his followers lined up to receive the
token payment of five dollars and a few simple provisions like
flour, lard, and tea. Seen one way, this annual ceremony served to
benefit the servants of the other institutions of the small outpost,
both the traders and the missionaries. The people now had one
more reason to appear at the growing settlement and thereby fall
under the influence of Church and trade. The priest, in particular,
expressed initial ambivalence toward this situation, as recorded
in the *Codex historicus*. "This became an occasion for them to
come each year to the Mission. The missionaries did not allow
this occasion to pass without taking advantage of the great bene-
fits that could result for these Christians of the Mission." But then
a few years later, reflecting perhaps some greater insight, the
codex reads:

> The painful days of the Treaty passed with the government
> Commission arriving to us, like all the years since 1907, at the
> end of July. These are not days of peace and repose, not for
> the bodies, nor for the souls. The "allmighty dollar" begins to
> awaken the passions in our savages that has lain dormant in
> their hearts and has not been there for a very long time. . . .
> Effects of the treaty on our savages, more bad than good. The
> effects of the government goods over the years on the savages of
> the treaty are a source of quarrels and disputes between them.

And the next year it reads: "I wish I could paint these days to give
them their true colour, to show the foolhardiness of this enterprise.
Suffice it to say that these days were numbered among those of
which we do not want to speak. They were not pleasant."

The two bands remained attached to Lac du Brochet for many
years, but in time both moved on. The Lac la Hache Band, true to
its name and its earlier origins, moved northwest to the shores of
Wollaston Lake (also known as Lac la Hache), closer to its traditional hunting and trapping territory. The Dene of the Barren
Land Band were eventually overwhelmed in Lac du Brochet by
the influx of Cree from the south, largely brought about by Cree

involvement in the freighting of supplies up Reindeer Lake. As the Cree outnumbered the Dene in what by then was simply known as Brochet, the Dene retreated to the north toward their traditional territory and formed a new band called the Northlands Band. Today, strangely, the Barren Land Band is almost entirely Cree, made up of people who are not at all from the barrenlands. The Dene, once proudly led by Casimir, perhaps the most renowned chief of all time in the region, established a new community in the late 1970s—with no government assistance—on the shores of the next lake to the north, which, just to confuse the issue further, is known as Lac Brochet.

❧ ❧ ❧ ❧ ❧

As I walk along the shore of Brochet in the spring of 2005, past the venerable mission, past the old HBC post, and up onto the flat tableland dotted with modern if simple bungalows, I'm enveloped by a sense of a community that history has passed over but which nevertheless remains attached to its heritage, proud of a past unlike any other. The dwellings are arranged in different areas according to the affiliation of the occupants: the Treaty 10 signatories on reserve land in one section, most of them Cree or Métis; the nontreaty people in another section; and notably, the one remaining Dene family out at the farthest end of town to the north, as if the location were symbolic. I'm headed for a tidy little house set back in a grove of jack pine where eighty-five-year-old Philomene Umpherville lives. It is a cold, gray day in late April. The temperature is twenty-eight degrees Fahrenheit, much colder with the windchill. I have my fur cap pulled down over my ears and my winter anorak's collar turned up against the strong northwesterly gusts. It's a good day to sit inside over tea at Philomene's kitchen table. She has some stories to tell me. And I have some of Oberholtzer's old photographs to show her.

Memories

In the old photograph, taken by Oberholtzer in 1912 outside St. Pierre's church in Lac du Brochet, a proud-looking Dene man stands in a vested suit and a wide-brimmed Stetson beside but just apart from half a dozen young boys. The Dene man is Alphonse Dzeylion. Presumably, the Mass had only just finished, presided over by Fr. Egenolf. Ernest Oberholtzer, the tourist, had attended the Mass and was set to embark on a photographic walkabout through the community with Alphonse.

▷ ▷ *Sunday July 28. It was a beautiful warm clear morning. Father Egenolf brought me a special chair and prayer table to kneel on and I sat at the back of the church, where I could see all the Indians at worship. The women and children sat on benches or on the floor to the left. The men in their wrinkled clothes and with their heads of black straight hair bows sat to the right. Now and then a child crossed over to its father or a worried mother left the church with her squawking papoose. Once there was an audible sound of nursing. Nearly all the women seemed to have colds and some kept spitting. One very wrinkled old woman on the floor was stroking the head of a very fat, bashful, babyish boy that lay in her lap. Several of the children were clean and pretty, the worst two were daughters of one mother, fat, dull, troublesome and filthy dirty. The women all wore shawls on their heads, black, striped-red, and gray; several wore dresses with neat tucks of green or blue round the skirts. When all the people had come in and crossed themselves with holy water from the conker shell at the door, the service began. Two altar boys, tinkling of bells, censers. An intermittent wheezing turned out to be an organ, with Alphonse presiding. The voiceless voices of the squaws. Service books in syllabic Chipewyan and illustrated. The thud of the flat mocassined feet when the Indians were leaving after they had taken communion. The rude equipment and decorations of the church. Stations of the cross, bunting, paper stained-glass, crucifix.*

He took other striking photographs of people in Lac du Brochet, most notably of two groups of women including Elyse Cook, Eugenie Cook, Eliza Cook, and Marie Cook, all of them Philomene Umpherville's relatives (see photo, p.38). Her mother was Catherine Cook. The women in the photos are her aunts and cousins.

⌄   ⌄   ⌄   ⌄   ⌄

Philomene (née Lapensée) was born in 1920 in Lac du Brochet. Her father was Adolphe Lapensée, manager of the HBC post. Twice widowed, he married her mother, his third wife, a year before when he was thirty-eight. Catherine Cook, a Métis woman with strong Red River Settlement and fur trade roots, whose family was then living in Lac du Brochet, was eighteen. Philomene was the first born of this union, although she had older half-siblings from the previous marriages. Her family heritage is the embodiment of the region's history, the opening of the north, the fur trade, and the interactions of early traders with "country wives." Philomene herself, while very humble and kindhearted by nature, somehow stands apart, rising above the crowd in Brochet. She expresses pride at being "nontreaty" yet speaks Cree fluently, English well, and some Chipewyan and French—"I used to speak good French, but no one speaks French here now," so she lost it. She is proud above all of her Cook family's Métis ancestry.*

Her maternal grandfather, Joseph Cook, worked for the HBC (his immediate supervisor, therefore, was Philomene's father, Adolphe Lapensée), which provided his family with sufficient affluence to live in one of the six two-storey log houses in their settlement. Philomene is clearly proud as she recalls the house, its curtained

---

* In this case her use of "Métis" to describe the Cooks refers to a mix of Cree and English Protestant (i.e., HBC trader) stock.

windows, its separate bedrooms upstairs with "fancy" iron beds, and its well-equipped kitchen with "beautiful cast iron frying pans" and "nice dishes." Remarkably, the family line can be traced back through a succession of HBC employees to a lad recruited in England in the late eighteenth century. Philomene's great-great-great-great-grandfather, William Hemmings Cook, was born about 1766 in London, of Anglican parents. At age twenty he signed on with the HBC and took passage to York Factory where he began his career as a clerk. He rose through the ranks steadily, spending much of his time inland helping to establish and manage the company's developing network of trading posts. At age forty-four in 1810, he was appointed chief factor at York Factory, with an annual salary of one hundred pounds, plus a profit-sharing bonus. In all he had sixteen children from three wives. His first wife was Kahnapawanakan, a Cree woman whose son Joseph Cook is Philomene's great-great-great-grandfather. (The names Joseph and William appear repeatedly in the family tree.) Like his father before him and the seven generations that followed, he worked for the HBC, including a stint as the assistant trader at Cumberland House in 1814. The tradition continued uninterrupted. His namesake, Philomene's grandfather, was similarly employed when she was born in 1920.

When Chief Factor William Cook retired from the HBC in 1819, he joined the newly arrived Red River settlers in their struggle to fulfill Lord Selkirk's dream of establishing a new colony in the west. He received a land grant of five hundred acres where he lived out his days until his death at age eighty in 1846. His heirs remained in the region, worked for the HBC, and served at posts across the Northwest. The family's story reflects the history of the opening up of the country along the old travel route from Winnipeg to The Pas to Reindeer Lake.

When Adolphe Lapensée arrived in the Northwest to enter service with the HBC, he was a complete greenhorn, compared with the family into which he would ultimately marry. Born in the French-speaking community of Plantagenet, Ontario, in 1881, his first posting with the HBC was as clerk at Cumberland House in 1904. After two years he left the company to become a schoolteacher in the growing community, where he stayed until 1917, at which point he moved his growing family—by this time he had a second wife and six children—to Lac du Brochet, where he resumed employment with the HBC. By 1919, he was married for the third time and had been promoted to HBC manager. The next year, Philomene was born, and two years after that, he left the HBC to work independently.

Lapensée moved his family sixty miles north, up the Cochrane River, to a spot called Sandy Hills, where he established his own little trading post. The white fox trade was just hitting its stride, and there was money to be made by both trapper and trader. The location was designed to intercept the Dene and Inuit on their way down to trade at Lac du Brochet. Philomene's earliest childhood memories are of this place. "I liked it there. It was a beautiful place." Her father built a comfortable house, and she played with children from the Chipewyan camp across the river, where about ten families lived. "In the winter, sliding and snowshoeing, and getting wood with the dog teams. And in the summer time we had a little tent. . . . Even I used to cook some bannock, outside just, I remember." Life in the bush was good.

It was a busy little post. "People came because it was closer, from the north. My Dad had some clothing, and flour, baking powder, lard, tea, sugar," and many more trade items. In return, over the winter he accumulated sufficient fur that each summer he made a trip down to Winnipeg to sell his fur. In the early years he made the trip by canoe, paddling, or sailing when the wind cooperated. But business was good enough that before long Lapensée became the first person in Brochet to own an outboard motor, a five-horsepower Evinrude. Philomene remembers a few years later traveling down Reindeer Lake by motorboat, head held high, not even looking at the canoes paddling along as she and her father passed by quickly and noisily.

At Sandy Hills, though she played with the Dene children on

Government surveyor C. S. MacDonald (left),
*with Adolphe Lapensée at his Sandy Hills trading post
beside the Cochrane River, in 1924.*

occasion, her family maintained a comfortable distance. Philomene grew up feeling apprehensive about some aspects of the unfamiliar culture, especially the dancing to drums and rattles that she observed in the camp across the river. One time, she recalls, with a glint of humor in her eye, her father was unable to sleep because of the racket drifting across the river in the middle of the night. He looked out to see a big fire and, in the light of the flames, some Dene men dancing around to the beat of the drums. Then it stopped, suddenly, and he wondered why. Minutes later, the Dene arrived at his doorstep, terrified, having packed up their camp in a great rush and paddled across the river to warn their friend the trader that the *windigo* had come to visit and that he too should flee.* A short time after their hasty departure, two Cree trappers, well known to Lapensée, arrived at his house, and the explanation unfolded. The men were returning from their spring trapping in

---

* *Windigo*, or sometimes *wetigo*, is a Cree word referring to a spirit.

the North, coming down the Cochrane River in their canoe. When they saw the dancing by firelight at the Dene camp, they decided to have some fun, so they beached their canoe, snuck quietly through the trees in the dark toward the camp, and threw a stick toward the revellers. Panic ensued. The Dene jumped to the immediate conclusion that a *windigo* was lurking in the shadows, fearfully struck camp, and took flight. The Cree men watched with delight and then returned to their canoe and paddled over to Lapensée's cabin to share a laugh.

In 1930, when Philomene was ten, Lapensée decided to move his family back to Brochet so that his children could be educated. Though he continued to operate his trading post at Sandy Hills with some help, his family took up residence in a new log cabin in town that he built not far from the HBC post. Philomene remembers that house and those times fondly. "I used to live down by the lake and get my water by chopping a hole through the ice, three feet thick. Not like now." To underline her point, she points at the hot and cold water taps in her modern kitchen. "There was just cabins [then], some of them were beautiful. The good workers had gardens: potatoes, carrots, onions, beets. In the springtime we were in a hurry to plant the garden, hungry for those vegetables. We had a [root cellar] to keep the vegetables. Br. Drouin, from Quebec, and Fr. Egenolf, they had a beautiful garden."

Most of the children in the settlement went to school, taught by Br. Drouin mostly in Cree, with a bit of French thrown in. "In the morning, before we went to school, we carried three or four pieces of wood to the school. Every child did so. That way we had enough to heat the school. We were strong. It was a good life. Years ago, we helped each other. There was no money involved. We were happy."

Brochet was changing, and life at the frontier was changing with it. The dedicated brother at the mission now had anywhere from fifteen to thirty Métis children to teach. More and more families were building cabins and putting down roots. Most of the Cree and some of the Dene children went south to a residential school.

Most of the Dene families were still living more closely connected to the land, less inclined to adopt the ways of settlement life. Groceries from the south were now arriving more regularly, however, often by plane. Philomene remembers the first time an airplane landed on Reindeer Lake in front of the town. It was so noisy, she said, that the old people were frightened. One elderly man ran to the priest as the plane was roaring down toward the lake, its wings outstretched just above the water, screaming, "Father, it's Jesus coming down on the cross!"

In 1938, when Philomene was eighteen, Lapensée decided to take his children to Plantagenet, Ontario, for more education. Philomene completed grade ten there before leaving school to get a job and help support the family. When the Second World War ended, she and her sister Vicki decided they wanted to go back west. The two young women got on the train in Ottawa, Philomene with four hundred dollars in her pocket, and headed west to The Pas. There they found jobs at the Roman Catholic hospital working, as she remembers, seven to seven, presumably as nursing assistants, and being paid forty dollars a month plus room and board. At a party for some soldiers just returning from the war, Philomene met Albert Umpherville, one of the many dashing young uniformed heroes. They fell in love and were married a few months later, notwithstanding his mother's disapproval of Philomene's being both French and Catholic. Not a year later, they were back in Brochet, Philomene having declared she would live nowhere else. Initially, Albert eked out a living as a trapper, a fisherman, and a sometime motor mechanic, until ultimately running the local Manitoba Hydro power plant. Philomene worked mostly as a cook, though she also nursed a long-term patient through the palliative care stage. They had five children, worked hard to support their family, and managed to get by.

Things changed somewhat in 1978 when Philomene discovered a market for one of her greatest talents. As a young girl she had learned to sew, to prepare raw moose hide, and to do decorative beadwork. Both her mother and her grandmother were accomplished seamstresses, embroiderers, and quill workers, and her aunt, her mother's sister, taught her to use beads. So she came by her skills quite naturally. She became famous in her own right for her beadwork and sold as much as she could produce. When Pope John Paul II visited Canada and held a special Mass for the Native peoples, he was presented with one of Philomene's works of art, a beaded cross on white caribou hide. She was once commissioned to make a pair of beaded white caribou slippers for Queen Elizabeth II. And somehow Walt Disney acquired a pair of gauntlet mitts made by her—she has his thank-you note to prove it. Her failing eyesight and arthritic fingers no longer permit the fine work, but before she stopped producing, she made moccasins, belts, vests, and mitts for every member of her large family. They, like everyone else who has been lucky enough to meet her, will never forget Philomene Umpherville.

▿   ▿   ▿   ▿   ▿

Just minutes away from Philomene's house, set back against the trees on the opposite side of the road, live Jean Baptiste "J. B." Merasty and his wife, Therese. The man standing to one side in several of Oberholtzer's photographs, the man whom Oberholtzer tried to hire as a guide for one dollar a day, Alphonse Dzeylion, is Therese's father. She stares at the youthful image of her father from twelve years before she was born. She is mesmerized. J. B. talks.

Jean Baptiste "J. B." Merasty, Brochet, 2005.

He recalled life in Brochet when he was just a boy in the 1920s. He remembers the HBC buying caribou for five dollars each during its operation as a meat post. They kept the frozen caribou over the winter and then in the spring hired local women to cut up and dry the meat and pound it into pemmican, for which they were paid one dollar a day. Mostly, though, J. B. talked of the old medicine, or *įk'ózį* (pronounced "inkonze"), of encounters with Inuit, and of the most amazing events he'd witnessed during his long life. He is old enough to remember well the freighting by York boat and the days when the annual supplies arrived in late summer in a much anticipated, small armada of boats rowing up Reindeer Lake.

> People were scared when the freighters were away. There used to be a lot of older people that knew *ık̓ózı̨*, the old medicine. As summer passed, people at Brochet worried about the York boat crew, thinking of the hard trip. They worried, what if someone was sending them bad medicine. The HBC would send a party of three men, including a shaman, out to meet the returning York boat at Southend. The shaman would help them find the freighters. They'd build him a small tipi and he'd go in there and dream, to find out where the York boat was.
>
> When the old man was in the tipi, they could hear two men talking, as he found out where the York boat was, on its way home, talking to the boat captain. It had to be a strong tipi, because he had strong power.

J. B. also remembers Casimir, the man who was elected chief of the Idthen-eldeli when the treaty was signed in 1907.

> This old man was actually killed by his dog team. He hit his head and died. I think there was a tree across his trail and he hit his head. He was a good man. I remember seeing him.
>
> A long time ago, when caribou came back from north in the fall, Casimir was one of the best hunters, with spear, at river crossings. He used to have the medicine power. He used to cure people. Through this power, he helped people. I saw one man that he had cured.
>
> There was a man, Adam Halkett, a Cree, that was very sick. Someone sent him bad medicine. He was about to die. He sent for Casimir. This was up at Kasmere Lake [as it is now known, actually named after Casimir]. Casimir went into the tent. We heard the two men talking, because Casimir knew some Cree. As he went in the tent, Casimir had nothing, no medicine, just his bare hands. Adam could barely move. Casimir opened up Adam's shirt buttons and sucked on him everywhere. Few minutes later, Adam got up and walked out of the tent, saying thank you to Casimir.

As a young man traveling widely and living as a hunter and a trapper, J. B. recalls meeting Inuit. He has several memories of these encounters.

> One time an Inuit family, the parents and three children, came to Brochet by dog team in the spring time. They stayed for the summer and left after freeze-up in the fall. But the Inuit wanted to leave one boy, about four or five, here in Brochet with Solomon Cook. Solomon really loved that little Inuit boy. Next spring he took him duck hunting at Philip's Bay, nearby here, a good place for ducks. When they met some other [Dene] hunters, Solomon asked the boy to get some wood for a fire, to make tea. He walked off into the woods. A little while later, Solomon got worried about him and started looking. Then all the men were searching the woods and everywhere. Finally they gave up and decided he must have drowned after falling into the water.
>
> That summer men from here were hired by the HBC to freight trade goods up north. On their trip they met Casimir and he travelled with them. They came across a camp of Inuit. Casimir could speak some Inuit. They thought they saw that little Inuit boy. Casimir asked and he said, "Yes, it's me." When they asked how he was returned to his family, the boy said he remembered going into the woods for firewood. Then he saw an Inuit man who called him over, then picked him up and suddenly they were back at his family's camp.

⌄   ⌄   ⌄   ⌄   ⌄

Įk̓ózį, in its simplest form, is likened to shamanism. But it was much more than that. It is rarely discussed today, but informants such as J. B. Merasty confirm that people with this power used it for healing, through sweat lodges and the drum and also through dreaming. These people were visionaries and mystics who served as doctor, guide, and interpreter of events for their people.

Among the Dene there is a legendary figure by the name of Bërgházeh, imbued by Dene account with almost magical powers. He acquired this knowledge and ability, it is told, during a visit to an Inuit camp. Details of the specific process vary. By one account, from a man named Julien Toulejour (born in 1888, died in 1982), Bërgházeh traveled with his uncle to an Inuit camp farther north, probably near the upper reaches of the Kazan River. In the camp was an Inuit couple whose only son had just died.

> People used to go to the Eskimos for things. When Bërgházeh was small he went with his uncle to an Eskimo place.
>
> How did he learn that? Well, when he came inside their house, the Eskimo man said, "Come here my son." So Bërgházeh went and sat between the Eskimo man and his wife. He didn't understand their language [at that time]. But the Eskimo man asked the Dene how long they were going to stay. They said "Four days."
>
> So that Eskimo man said, "I will give my son what I use to live. He will stay with me for four days, then I will give him back to you."
>
> When they were going to bed the Eskimo man put Bërgházeh's head against his neck and that's where he slept and dreamt. But it was not the strong *ɂkʼózɨ*. Bërgházeh was scared but he did not wake up. He wouldn't wake up unless the Eskimo man woke him up. When he woke up in the morning, when he got up, "These medicines were like I made them myself," said Bërgházeh. "There were other things too that I knew," he said. "I was talking in their Eskimo language too when I got up in the morning. I know how they live, what they eat, everything, by dreaming." That's where he learned *ɂkʼózɨ*, from the Eskimos.

Bërgházeh, it is said, could cross even the roughest wind-tossed waters in his boat without fear of being upset. A Dene elder, Elzear Herman, cited a man who had watched as "Bërgházeh set out in his birch bark canoe and out in the lake he went. The storm was. very bad and the wind was strong. But for several feet on both sides of the canoe the water was calm and Bërgházeh had no trouble getting across." His powers were extensive. He healed the sick. He protected his people from evil. He used his magic to control and even kill those who harmed others. When he died, many years ago now but within living memory for many Dene elders, a loon flew out from under his pillow and landed on the lake. He was, some said, the last man to have *įk'ózį*. J. B. Merasty does not agree, however. "Some people still have that power and use it," he said at the end of many long hours of spellbinding storytelling.

⌄   ⌄   ⌄   ⌄   ⌄

Annie Benonie, a devout Roman Catholic, says that when her father, Alphonse Dzeylion, died in 1938, he got sick in the spring and remained ill for some months. The family took him to their fishing camp, thinking he could die soon. "When he took his last breath, a bug of some kind crawled out of his nose. When this happened, the old people knew he had died by bad medicine, from *įk'ózį*. We didn't know who had done *įk'ózį* on him." He was fifty-four years old.

She remembers him proudly as a strong Catholic, a skilled carpenter who helped build the church in Brochet, and a good man. When he was still young, he was among a small group of Dene who traveled north one winter when word reached the Lac du Brochet post that some Inuit in the barrenlands were starving. The men decided to take meat up to the Inuit. Four Inuit came back south with the Dene party and stayed in Lac du Brochet through the spring and summer. They built kayaks using caribou skins, and as summer approached its end, they left again for the north.

Annie Benonie also remembers Casimir, the first elected chief, who, it is said by some, had the power of *įk'ózį*. The stories about him suggest, rather, that he was an extremely powerful and strong-willed figure who ruled over his people with firmness, kindness, and wisdom. If missionaries suggested he employed the "bad medicine," it may have had more to do with his ambivalence toward the Church and his hesitation to spend any more time than necessary within the sphere of their influence. Annie Benonie describes him as a good provider who held onto traditional Dene beliefs and spent most of his time in the North, often farther north than most, right on the edge of the barrenlands.

Casimir's grandson, Alfred Denechezhe, when he was nearly ninety, recalled the wisdom of his grandfather. "At that treaty signing, when government offered money, he didn't want to accept it. He said it would bring problems in the future." Some Dene think he showed profound foresight. Casimir became the chief, according to his grandson, who remembers traveling on his grandfather's dogsled, because he knew how to survive and he was able to lead his people to where they could find caribou.

After several years as chief, Casimir demanded at the annual gathering that the Indian agent provide his people with new canoes. When the government refused his request, Casimir refused the government's money. The standoff persisted for another year and then a third. The Indian agent solved the problem by appointing a new chief, giving him the money, and thereby ending Casimir's tenure as chief. Casimir left town in a huff, heading north, and kept himself and his large family away from the post (and the mission, much to the disappointment of Fr. Egenolf) for years to follow. He may have no longer been the chief, but Casimir continued to guide the Idthen-eldeli in the all-important matter of finding and hunting caribou.

Casimir lived into old age. Before he died in the winter of 1939 to 1940, he told his people he wanted to be buried standing up, on a hillside, looking out across the water of the travel route he knew so well, the old way north. His grave is on a sand hill on the south side of the narrows in Fort Hall Lake. He wanted to watch his people going north to hunt caribou in the manner of their ancestors, in the pursuit of a way of life he must have known could not go on forever but which he must have hoped would not be lost so long as his final wish was remembered.

5

Into the Beyond

▷ ▷ *Monday, July 29. I said good-bye to the priest, who still suggested*
that I engage [another guide], and then at nearly six o'clock on a
beautiful clear evening Billy and I set out for the river. We paddled
on till nearly ten o'clock before we reached the high sandy portage
at the first big rapid. We camped at the far end.

Oberholtzer and Magee were on their way again, on their own,
cloaked in more uncertainty than even they knew. They were now
camped near the mouth of the Cochrane River where it flows into
Reindeer Lake. Lying ahead was the task of ascending the swift
current to the point where they would leave the river, portage over
a height of land, and begin their descent toward the barrenlands of
Oberholtzer's dreams, still two hundred miles or more to the north.

They had left behind Lac du Brochet, the last outpost, the last
source of outside assistance or sustenance they could count on.
Oberholtzer had spent ten dollars to resupply with four pounds of
beans, ten pounds of pork, fifteen pounds of hardtack, and five
pounds of sugar at this humble post. A traveler just two years
later, Captain Angus Buchanan, recorded this impression.

> The small, log-hewn, square-built cabins are weather-beaten
> and gray like time-worn boulders on the wayside, and stand as
> solitary as sentinels on a bare, treeless, grass grown knoll. The
> Fort—the buildings of the Hudson Bay Company—comprising
> a house, a trading store, and an assortment of outhouses—
> stands dominant on the highest ground on the east of the knoll.
> To the west, strange to say, is a tiny Catholic mission and
> church: the latter cross-planned as is the Roman custom, not-
> withstanding its insignificant size and crude workmanship. At
> some distance is the trading store of the "French Company"
> (Revillon Brothers), rival traders to the Hudson Bay Company,

who here established a footing some ten years ago. There are six cabins in the settlement occupied by part-blood or full-blood Indians, who are at intervals in summer and winter employed in the transport of furs and stores for the trading companies.

This was the scene that slowly disappeared in the wake of their solitary canoe as each paddle stroke carried them farther from the tiny outpost. Even this small source of comfort and respite, at the frontier, however insignificant, was now behind Oberholtzer and Magee as they struck off into the beyond. This was country well known by the Dene but traversed by only a handful of white men. Even the Mounties had not yet made it this far.

A Royal North West Mounted Police patrol report from 1915, written by Sgt. H. R. Handcock, offers an insight into the force's early activity in the area. It is important to remember that these men were as tough as nails, hardened and capable travelers, even in winter. On the patrol he is describing here, they covered a total of 1,851 miles by dog team over a period of fifty-seven days in midwinter.

> Arriving at the south end of Reindeer Lake on the 18th [of January] I decided to hire an Indian from here to help break trail as no sleighs had been over the lake since snow fell and we had had five days of very hard travelling. Taking it in turn to break trail our journey from this point [South End] to the Hudson's Bay Cos. Post on the north end of the lake [Lac du Brochet] was the usual hard grind, there being no road [trail]. The thermometer fell very low, to 60 degrees below zero we afterwards discovered, and with a north wind blowing, on such a large lake travelling was to say the least very unpleasant. However we arrived at the north end on Sunday 24th, having been on the lake for the best part of six days, and the dogs were quite footsore after their trip of 575 miles, 350 of which was breaking trail, taking 21 days from Isle a la Crosse, and 19 days actual travelling, averaging 30 miles per day.
>
> I stayed at Reindeer Lake some 16 days intending to patrol to the Esquimaux Post about 300 miles north of Reindeer Lake but had to give up the idea as I could see no way of making this

patrol without an expenditure of $200.00, it being necessary to take three trains of dogs, as dog food and rations have to be taken for the trip, there being no game en route, and having to figure on 24 days for the round trip at this time of year.

I left on February 9th to patrol to Barren Land Chipewyan camp 80 miles north, returning on the 12th after a very nice trip: good roads [trails] and good weather. I found the Indians (8 families) more or less healthy, very dirty, and [with] an abundance of meat. I rested my dogs three days and left on the 16th for Indian camp 75 miles north east having a good trip and seeing herds of countless caribou. I found the Indians (7 families) OK and returned on the 20th.

It was into this same country that Oberholtzer and Magee were now headed. They had the map prepared by Tyrrell after his 1894 expedition, and they had the sketch map drawn in Lac du Brochet with the assistance of the priest and local Dene men. Apart from that, they had to have confidence in their own abilities. "Billy said he thought we could find our way" was Oberholtzer's only real expression of this confidence, such as it was.

Over the next few days, the men slowly ascended the Cochrane River with a combination of paddling, portaging, lining, and wading. The weather for the most part was fair, and the travel, though laborious, was not that difficult. Once or twice they took a wrong turn, most often into a dead-end bay, and had to backtrack. Along the way they passed by Sandy Hills where ten years later Adolphe Lapensée would establish his small trading post. In 1912, he was still teaching school at Cumberland House.

After five days they reached the portage into Lac Brochet, where by coincidence they met a group of Dene men heading south in five canoes with a load of meat and pemmican for the trading post, some fifty or sixty miles downriver to the south. "In a moment we were completely surrounded by these men whom we had never seen before in our lives. And they acted very strangely," recalled Oberholtzer years later. "They surrounded us, and immediately began to look at our things. They opened some of my packs, and they didn't smile. They were very grave about the whole thing. So then I picked out the man that looked most like the chief.* He was a little fellow. I walked up to him, and handed him a part of a plug of tobacco, and held out my hand to shake hands, and he shook hands. Immediately it was all off—everybody smiled and laughed." Before long, Oberholtzer and Magee pushed off in their canoe onto the waters of Lac Brochet.

⊽   ⊽   ⊽   ⊽   ⊽

Lac Brochet is a fair expanse of open water, the site today of the most modern Dene village in the region, where the newly formed Northlands Band chose to build a new settlement in the late 1970s, anxious to escape what they perceived as excessive influence and control held by the Crees, Métis, and non-Natives in the old settlement of Lac du Brochet. Willie Loon, seventy years old now, remembers how it all happened.

He and two friends, all living in Lac du Brochet in 1970 (by then called simply Brochet), traveled north on a hunting trip by snowmobile in midwinter. They reached Lac Brochet before they saw any signs of caribou, but on the lake right beside where the tiny settlement now sits, they each shot four or five caribou. As they were skinning and gutting their catch—cold work in midwinter— they noticed a fire just a mile to the south, so they loaded up to go join whomever was there, "to share fire with him" and have some tea. Then they noticed a fresh dogsled trail leaving the lake ice and winding up into the woods, so the three men on their machines followed the trail. A short while later, they came back onto the lake to an island where Thomas Denechezhe had his cabin. He was living there all alone, an old man who had survived a long and difficult—typically Dene—life of hunting and trapping in the vast country to the north. He welcomed the visitors as a break from his solitude.

The three younger hunters planned to return to Brochet that night, even though it was now getting dark. "It was only three

---

* This was probably Casimir.

hours and we had headlights," explained Loon. But the old man persuaded them to stay. "Why leave?" he said. "The sun will come up in the morning." And sometimes when you rush, he pointed out, is when "things" happen. So the younger men took the elder's counsel and stayed overnight.

His spirits buoyed by the company, Thomas Denechezhe told story after story into the wee hours of the night. His three visitors were enthralled by his tales of survival in "the country." He recounted one occasion when he went out looking for food for his starving family, walking on snowshoes because some of his dogs had already starved to death. Finally, after walking all day, as Dene had been doing for centuries, he found some caribou and shot a few. By the time he finished skinning and butchering the caribou, it was dark, and Denechezhe was exhausted. He prayed that his children would survive another night without food. Before sleeping, he formed one of the fresh caribou skins into a rough toboggan shape, curved up at the front and curled up on either side, so it would freeze overnight. The other skins he used for warmth as he slept out in the open. In the morning he loaded up his makeshift toboggan with fresh meat, tied a rope on the front, and started the long walk back to his family, pulling a heavy load of life-saving meat. He made it. They all survived. Even the remaining dogs regained sufficient strength to help move the family's camp north to where Denechezhe had found the caribou. Ever since then, he said, his family had always had enough to eat. Without saying as much, Denechezhe clearly credited the location.

After a night of stories, the three young Dene hunters loaded up their toboggans and returned to their families in Brochet. But the seed was planted in their minds. Three years later, twelve Dene families from Reindeer Lake decided to reestablish farther north on the shores of Lac Brochet, exactly on the point where Willie Loon and his hunting companions had found their caribou and only a mile or so from Denechezhe's cabin. They built their own log cabins, plus a small school for their children, and recruited a non-Dene friend to come and live with them to serve as the teacher. Five years after that, the government decided to build some more houses, and several additional families moved up from the larger town at Brochet. In 1980, the new settlement achieved reserve status, and the Northlands Band was officially established on the shores of Lac Brochet. Now it is a modern village of friendly people, a tiny cluster of attractive houses with a school that could win prizes for architectural design. Known simply as Lac by the locals, its very existence is a reflection of the nomadic roots and fierce independence of the Idthen-eldeli.

⌄ ⌄ ⌄ ⌄ ⌄

From here Oberholtzer and Magee faced mostly lake travel to ascend the Cochrane River to its most northern point, and there the old way north makes a giant leap, from the waters flowing generally through southern and central Canada and over a height of land into the waters flowing generally through northern Canada. This portage was never part of the early voyageurs' route, so it bears no memorable name, reflecting neither ignominy nor celebration, like Grand Portage, Methye Portage, or even Frog Portage. Arguably, it is every bit as significant in history, as a critical juncture in a well-trodden route so essential to the country's heritage.

The portage out of the river leads to a chain of small lakes heading north and eventually into the headwaters of the Thlewiaza River. Transiting the chain of lakes in early August, Oberholtzer's greatest excitement came from repeated sightings of caribou. This was not surprising, of course. The reason Dene had used this travel route for centuries was to access the country where the caribou abound during summer months.

This stretch of their route, one can infer, provided Oberholtzer and Magee with the halcyon days of their long journey. They were beyond the frontier, where the explorer in Oberholtzer had dreamed of going. He had every reason to feel that this, at last, was the wilderness he sought, that very few feet had trod where his now did, and those few that had were almost all wearing moccasins. On August 5, revelling in the experience, Oberholtzer wrote: "All the portages, of which we made three more, were easy to find and perfect for walking, even barefoot." The vast land around them was all but empty of other human beings. They were surrounded by caribou. The fish were biting. The weather was warm, the sun shone, and the wind for the most part was at their backs. Two canoeists could ask for nothing more. Though they carried a rifle, they chose not to hunt for meat. Surely, had Alphonse Dzeylion consented to guide their trip from Brochet north, Oberholtzer and Magee would have now been sitting around a fire watching some sizzling caribou ribs, suspended on a birch sapling, dripping fat into the fire.

On August 6, they reached Thanout Lake, at least part of which is now called Fort Hall Lake. Of the narrows between the lakes two major bodies, Oberholtzer recorded: "At the top-most point some Indian has built a new conical lookout of spruce trees, from which he can see the surrounding country for miles." That is where Casimir was buried some years later, on the hilltop, standing up. But in 1912, Casimir was still very much in command of the Barren Land Band and still sporting his navy blue captain's jacket at the annual gathering for Treaty Day in Lac du Brochet. Near the north end of the lake, Oberholtzer noted seeing "several well built hewn-log houses of the Red Head family" but made no mention of seeing any people there, only a dog. Redhead himself had been dead for more than a decade at this time. This was near the site of his small trading post, to which he freighted goods from Lac du Brochet and at which he operated a successful business by trading with both Dene and Inuit. He was a man ahead of his time.

Rather than Redhead's camp, what Oberholtzer probably saw were the remains of a post called Fort Hall, built by Herbert Hall and adjacent to the former site of Redhead's camp on the east side of the lake. Between 1906 and 1908, Hall, working for the Hudson's Bay Company, had pushed the trade north by establishing this post beside Thanout Lake; another depot known as Canoe Limit, or Husky Portage, much farther to the north—but reachable by canoe and portage for freighting purposes—on Putahow Lake; and a third known as Eskimo Post at Ennadai Lake on the Kazan River, for which access required an overland trip, usually accomplished by dog team.

Nearly a month before, on July 11 at Pelican Lake, Oberholtzer had seen Herbert Hall and his brother Gordon on their way south with a load of furs. Herbert was in a boat out in midlake, traveling under sail, so Oberholtzer did not actually meet him. Gordon, however, took the time to talk on shore before he paddled on, informing the relative novice that "the route was bad, and there were no men to be had." As if this was not discouraging enough, Oberholtzer recorded that "this young man had done all he could to dissuade me from attempting the trip to Chesterfield," apparently to no avail, though one wonders if the seed thus planted was not growing still, even as the determined Oberholtzer was paddling by the post on Thanout Lake without even stopping to inspect in Herbert's absence. What Oberholtzer could not have known is that Fort Hall represented the beginning of a development yet to come, of heightened trading activity in the region immediately to the north and a proliferation of small trading posts in the country that Oberholtzer so much wanted to see before other white men arrived. The Fort Hall post continued operations into the 1930s, and the building remained sound for many years after that. A canoeist who visited the site in 1980 described his considerable excitement at seeing "the bleached and ancient Fort Hall trading post still standing. The living quarters were almost complete, with sand and moss still covering some of the roof-poles, and the beautifully-jointed heavy timbers of the front part still intact, although the roof had collapsed."

Herbert Hall and his brother Gordon were sons of HBC chief factor R. H. Hall. Herbert, by far the more renowned of the two, was described by fellow fur trader Alex Stevenson as "a giant of a man, over six feet tall and weighing nearly 300 pounds," and by another, Philip Godsell, as a "curly-haired, good-natured giant who boasted native blood on his mother's side [and who] was really one of the finest travellers and explorers that the Arctic had ever seen." There are legends told of his remarkable strength, of lifting a forty-five-gallon fuel drum singlehanded, of pulling a dog team up a mountain slope out of harm's way as an avalanche thundered past, and of surviving impossible conditions during some of his Arctic travels.

Leaving Fort Hall behind was, for Oberholtzer and Magee, a significant moment, more significant than they probably knew. They were, in effect, leaving behind their contact with the world they knew, forsaking any possibility of another encounter with other non-Native travelers, striking off, whether they knew it or not, into the beyond.

◁ ▷   ◁ ▷   ◁ ▷   ◁ ▷   ◁ ▷   ◁ ▷   ◁ ▷   ◁ ▷   ◁ ▷

A Modern Paddler's Perspective

Bill Layman is a devoted wilderness canoeist who lives in northern Saskatchewan. Fifteen years ago, he paddled out of Brochet for the first time, following the old way north to Nueltin Lake and beyond. He was hooked. He has returned to that same country, together with his partner, Lynda Holland, on several occasions since. Nearly every summer brings them back. In the beginning, he said, "I met the Cree, and they shared their stories with me. Later the Dene, and then the Inuit, did the same. Tied through bloodlines to the rhythms of the land, they were glad to talk to us about our trips. To them Lynda and I will be eternally grateful." His canoe trips in the land of the little sticks and out onto the barrenlands have prompted a thirst for a knowledge of those who went before: Cree, Dene, trappers and traders, early explorers and adventurers. "Without early travelers like Oberholtzer and Magee," said Layman, "the vibrancy of this region would be lost to those of us who follow, seeking our own adventures and hearing the echoes of those who have preceded us." Perhaps no modern-day paddler knows this route so well as Bill Layman does.

North on the Cochrane River to Fort Hall Lake
by Bill Layman

Paddling north on the Cochrane River from Brochet, Manitoba, you leave the Boreal Shield ecozone of Reindeer Lake and enter that of the Taiga Shield. In the Taiga Shield the plants and animals of two worlds—the boreal forest and the Arctic—meet and merge. The southern world slowly gives way to the northern as you paddle upstream on the Cochrane, deeper and deeper into what the Dene call "the land of little sticks."

You leave behind the giant inland ocean that is Reindeer Lake for the warm embrace of an easily followed route, where it is uncommon to be windbound or lost in a maze of islands and deceptive dead-end bays. What is astonishing is how quickly the landscape changes. Dense, mature forests of giant white spruce and balsam fir gradually thin over the two hundred odd kilometers along Reindeer Lake. Rocky shorelines and islands littered with sharp angled boulders slowly give way to a softer, sandy landform. Entering the Cochrane

"The land of little sticks" beside the Cochrane River.

River is like leaving one world behind for another that, if you are from southern Canada or the United States, is completely unknown.

Brochet sits directly on the edge of the Taiga Shield. From Brochet on north, it is a landscape of sand—not the rocky shield of Reindeer Lake and the Churchill River. Open forests of widely spaced jack pine and white birch rise above a carpet of caribou moss. Twinflower, bearberry, and Labrador tea predominate. The Dene and any who venture here call this parkland. And a true park it is—here you can walk for miles and not step over a dead tree. Poplar and balsam fir have mostly vanished and white spruce gives way to black spruce. Gray fire-killed jack pine firewood is everywhere and camping is easy on flat open table tops. Making note of "good campsites," as paddlers are wont to do in the boreal forest, is a waste of time here. When you need to stop for the day, a wonderful "fairyland" camp spot seems to always magically appear. Sandy-bottomed shallows thick with cattails, pond lilies, sedges and grasses lead to four and five foot high near-vertical banks of sand at shoreline's edge. There are no rocky, canoe-destroying boulder fields to fight here. Often as not, you can simply throw your gear up onto the bank and camp right where your pack lands, leaving your canoe floating and tied to a jack pine reaching out over the shoreline. Just off the edge of these high sandy parklands are low, wet bogs of black spruce, tamarack, willows, Labrador tea, and cloudberries.

Each day, paddlers will see tipped-over forests of gray weathered trees where forest fires have left mile after mile of rolling fire-scarred hillside. Here the underlayer is a dense maze of new growth: willow, alder, blueberries, white and dwarf birch, and purple fireweed growing up through a tangle of dead trees. Anyone unlucky enough to have to make a new portage through an area like this knows that walking here is as bad as it gets.

The Cochrane is less a river than a series of small- to medium-sized lakes— with names like Easton, Mahekan, Cann, and Thuycholeeni—that are joined by short, swift narrows. These narrows were scoured through the sandy ridges left by the Laurentide ice sheet that retreated from the landscape nearly ten thousand years ago. Here the tug of the Cochrane reminds you that you are on a river. Lac Brochet is the only large lake along the route.

There are rapids on the Cochrane, but they tend to be not so long and not nearly so violent as those found on the Churchill River. Portages are easy to find and provide excellent walking across dry, sandy ridges on well-packed trails. Portaging is supposed to be hard work, but with gentle sand put-ins and take-outs, no dense willows or tangled dead fall to fight, and no sucking, boot-stealing bogs, these almost seem like fun. These portages were once walked every summer by hundreds of Dene heading south to trade at Brochet and then back north to follow the herds of migrating caribou. Now summer travel is less common and is done by aluminum boats with outboards, not by canoe. But in winter snowmobiles use these same trails as people travel between the community of Brochet, on Reindeer Lake, and the newer community of Lac Brochet on the lake of the same name.

All along this magical river, campers are sung to sleep by the call of loons. In the morning they awake to the scolding of gray jays and the trill of white-throated sparrows. Every day, paddlers hear the array of migratory birds. Whether to nest or to simply feed and rest before winging off to their Arctic ranges, ducks, loons, geese, swans, and scores of other birds use the rich variety of habitat—from forest to lake to open sedge meadows to wetlands—all on offer in this area. Sightings of moose, black bear, otter, mink, fishers, beaver, and muskrat are frequent. Foxes and, more rarely, wolves can be seen. Fishing for pike and walleye at the bottom of rapids is sure to provide supper to hungry paddlers, and on some of the larger lakes, lake trout can be found in the deeper, colder water.

A not-so-welcome aspect of the country north of Brochet is the plague of blackflies, mosquitoes, and horseflies. Telling a Dene that what you remember of this country is *dejulie thon*—"lots of mosquitoes"—guarantees a knowing laugh. But this plague is the only real hardship and seems a fair price to pay to visit such a wonderful landscape.

One of the landmarks along the way is the old trading post at Sandy Hills, built by Adolphe Lapensée. Standing in the knee-high grass beside the one building still standing, it is easy to imagine parties of Dene camped across the river where they lived when they came to trade, or the winter igloos of Inuit on the river ice in front of the post.

In days gone by, as when Oberholtzer and Magee paddled this route, one might meet groups of Dene men and boys traveling in canoes en route to Brochet to trade or, earlier in the summer, find these same men and their families camped along the shores of the Cochrane. Now you might meet the descendants of these Dene who today live in Lac Brochet. From Lac they travel north, upstream on the Cochrane to summer cabins, sometimes venturing as far as the community of Wollaston Lake, where they visit friends and relatives. Less frequently, they venture south to the Cree community of Brochet.

The distance from Brochet to Kasmere Lake is 210 kilometres, much of it upstream work. Seven days, as Oberholtzer and Magee took, would seem a fairly easy pace for a modern paddler to maintain.

The portage from the Cochrane River into what P. G. Downes called "the chain of little lakes" is harder to find today than it used to be. Tucked behind a thick growth of willows and alder along a nondescript section of the Cochrane, in former times more obvious signs of travel would have been left by the northern Dene heading south by canoe. Today, the Dene of Lac Brochet no longer venture north by canoe in summer months. Neither do they use this portage in the winter as it is too steep for snowmobiles.

The trail today is still a steep climb up and over a high sand ridge that is covered with tall jack pine, followed by a mad scramble down a soft-sided sand hill into what Oberholtzer described as a "clear cold tarn," now called Lovell Lake. The hill down to the put-in is so steep that it is far easier to just let the canoe down with a rope than it is to carry it. Stately, tall white spruce rise from the end of the portage, stretching higher than the top of the steep hill. The view in all directions is of small blue lakes set among heavily burned, rolling sand hills. Great bald patches of white sand and gray armies of fire-killed trees cover the hillsides.

From the Cochrane River it is nearly thirty kilometers to Fort Hall Lake where, like all who have gone before, you finally join the Thlewiaza River. The ten dry, sandy, well-defined portages to Fort Hall Lake are more like roads than trails, linking a chain of three named lakes—Lovell, Smith House, and Blue—and six smaller unnamed lakes. The area is burned now as it was when Oberholtzer passed through, so the defining characteristic of this short section of the trip is sand—sand hills, sand beaches, firm sandy lake bottoms, sandy take-outs and put-ins, and sand portages. Camp spots are everywhere and are all much like those found on the Cochrane—dry, level parkland where it would be easy for a full Boy Scout troop to camp.

Just where you enter Fort Hall Lake, the charred remains of Pierre and Genevieve Besskkystare's trapping cabin can still be seen. Fort Hall Lake marks the beginning of the Thlewiaza River that enters into the lake from Hill House

Lake to the north. Fort Hall is a lake well known to the Dene. It is evident yet today that many lived here and many more passed through. Just to the north from the Besskkystares' burned home, an area of several acres on the western shore marks the remains of a huge Dene village, likely from the 1930s and 1940s. Now all that remains are fallen-in cabins and all manner of household and trapping gear—water pails, parts of sleighs, barrel stoves, snare wire, scraps of leather, stovepipes, and traps. Standing here in knee-high grass and sum-mer flowers, it is easy to think of the vibrant life that this land supported not so many years ago when the Dene were still nomadic: meat and fish on drying racks, the smell of wood smoke, women hauling water, others making hides for clothing, men huddled around a campfire trading stories and drinking tea. A lone man with his son and grandson might be paddling to the sand beach in front of the camp with a canoe full of jumbo whitefish. Perhaps another canoe of hunters might be returning from a hunt with fresh caribou meat or perhaps a moose. And from everywhere comes the noise of children finding a hundred ways to amuse themselves. This picture is sadly never to be seen again, but this image comes as close to reality as possible for a paddler standing on the shores of Fort Hall Lake, having ascended the Cochrane River and crossed the height of land into the upper reaches of the Thlewiaza River.

Midway along the lake is a sand narrows—perhaps one hundred meters across—with a sandy hill on the south side fronted by crescent-shaped sand beaches. If you walk to the top of this hill, you will find the fire-charred remains of a grave, the final resting place of the famous Dene chief Casimir. As was his wish, he was buried standing up on top of this hill, looking down so that he could see his people paddling north each year as they followed the caribou. They no longer come in summer, though Casimir still watches over his people as they pass by in the winter. Now, in summer, only paddlers visit, and often they stop to leave him some tea and dry meat if they have it.

6

Downstream at Last

▷ ▷ *August 7. I began to wade among the sharp hidden rocks, while*
Billy limped along the shore barefoot, sometimes holding the rope,
sometimes helplessly watching me. Again and again the canoe
nearly went smash on the countless rocks and as many times I went
in the cold water nearly to my waist.

The two intrepid travelers continued downstream on the Thlewiaza, though not without some difficulty. None of this seems to
have dampened Oberholtzer's enthusiasm for the expedition or
the country he was exploring. Of that same evening, he wrote:
"The sky was full of stars. At the first darkness, while the sky was
still luminous, it seemed as if the trees were all reflected by star-
light; then came a time just before moonrise when the shores
appeared as black masses only, without detail. Now and then
the aurora flared green across the sky and sent great reflected
streamers across the water." He sounds every bit a man who
remains enchanted by, and comfortable with, the natural environment he is experiencing.

The next morning, Oberholtzer realized the time for a momen-
tous decision had arrived. He was camped beside Theitaga, now
called Kasmere Lake, whence J. B. Tyrrell in 1894 headed north
and west to the headwaters of the Kazan River. This was the route
that Oberholtzer had read about, and had dreamed of following.
It is clear that right up to this moment that dream had not let go
its grip. "Having to decide whether to go on to Ennadai or to turn
east to the Thlewiaza, I told Billy to shave while I looked at my
maps." It was the morning of August 8. "The day was warm and
fair with wind still from the southwest." Perhaps that wind in-
fluenced his decision. He could head northwest, to follow Tyrrell,

paddle up a long arm of Kasmere Lake, then ascend the Little Partridge River, and from its headwaters cross a height-of-land into Kasba Lake, headwaters of the Kazan River. Or, by the alternate proposed to him in Lac du Brochet, he could let the fair wind carry him down the rest of Kasmere Lake to the point where the Thlewiaza flows out, headed for Hudson Bay—of that, he could be sure—though its exact course was largely uncharted.

One can be certain that Tyrrell's experience, on *his* first trip across the barrenlands, which found him fighting for his life on the shores of Hudson Bay in mid-September, was not far from Oberholtzer's thoughts on this day. Tyrrell was extraordinarily fortunate to escape alive. Now, for Oberholtzer, September was only slightly more than three weeks away. That would almost certainly mean the onset of wintry conditions. And from Tyrrell's report, Oberholtzer knew that the descent of the Kazan, and then working east to Hudson Bay by one route or another, would most certainly take more than three weeks, indeed five at a minimum. Notwithstanding the lure of following in the wake of his hero's canoe, it should have been an easy decision for anyone approaching the wilderness with just a modicum of respect and common sense. Accordingly, just three hours after arising from "a good rest under the stars," his decision was made. Oberholtzer and Magee "started off with the intention of going to Churchill," down the Thlewiaza, paddling their canoe to the northeast, rewarded with a tailwind down the length of Kasmere Lake. It was a decision that almost certainly saved their lives. And even at that, the trip ahead would prove to be anything but easy.

At the end of the lake, in the early afternoon, they came upon a Dene camp, notably all (about twenty) women and their children. It may well have been the camp of the men and boys, headed south for the annual treaty gathering, whom they had encountered five days after leaving the last outpost at the portage into Lac Brochet. Oberholtzer shook hands with the women, took their photographs, and engaged in trade. For four plugs of tobacco, he acquired a new pair of moccasins. "Everywhere meat

*The Dene camp beside Theitaga (Kasmere Lake)
visited by Oberholtzer and Magee on August 8, where
"everywhere meat was hanging to dry."*

was hanging to dry and a number of fat skin bags showed how it
was stored at least in the powdered form. A number of skins were
in the lake soaking for the tanning and others stretched tight on
the ground had been rubbed with the caribou brains which
looked like brown moss or clay." Had Alphonse Dzeylion consented to accompany Oberholtzer as a guide, how different the
experience of this visit, and earlier encounters, would have been.
Even more significant, perhaps, the Dene experience of the two
travelers from far away would have been entirely different.
Dzeylion would have explained that he was guiding this strange
pair—a *baunleye* (white man) and an *ena* (he would likely have
called Magee a Cree, as these women would have little or no
knowledge of Anishinaabe people). Imagine the looks of surprise
and wonder as he explained that they were going to the big water
of Hudson Bay and would surely see Eskimos. Such a journey
would be the stuff of legend to a nomadic people, perhaps alive
yet today in their oral history. Dzeylion's presence would have

unlocked doors of understanding for Oberholtzer; his experience (and journals) would be so much richer for it. As it was, the visit lasted only a few hours and was soon forgotten; by six o'clock their canoe was approaching the small rapid formed as the river flows out of Kasmere Lake.

Not more than a couple of miles on downstream, the pair stopped to make camp for the night, evidently still feeling quite relaxed about their pace and the distance to go. While making supper over a fire, a Dene man, whom Oberholtzer called Null-geh Josay U-gwan-i,* paddled up in his bark canoe. Evidently, his nearby camp was situated so as to intercept caribou, evidenced by the "long bloody-headed spear" in his "shallow kyack-like canoe." Oberholtzer and Magee were unable to speak with him, of course, but they "gave him some supper, matches, and a smoke, for which he seemed grateful." The next morning, prior to setting off down-river, they stopped in at Null-geh's camp, "pitched high on a barren rocky island, where the sun and wind could dry his meat." This would prove to be their last human contact before reaching Hudson Bay, still weeks away, though of course they had no way to know this.

▷ ▷ *Friday August 9. At the top, the family were sitting round a poor fire near which was a large iron kettle. Null-geh himself spread me a skin [to sit on] and as soon as I spied a pair of moccasins beside his wife, he handed them to me with a pair of bloody skin gloves. I got him half a pound of tea in return and some bits of tobacco. He seemed anxious to give me anything I liked but had no fresh meat. His own tent was full of skins and skin bags. He gave me the direction of the river, and then Billy and I set out.*

The dominant characteristic of the river for the next several miles, as recorded by Oberholtzer, was its rapids. Some they waded, some they lined, some they paddled, others they portaged. What is clear is that their sense of the trip was changing. "The prospects

* The better spelling is "Null-get."

for getting down the Little Fish [Thlewiaza] river looked blue," wrote Oberholtzer. Nor was the weather as agreeable as it had been. "All day it drizzled only stopping two or three times for five or ten minutes. The temperature was about 52° and there was no sun," he wrote on August 11. There were a few empty Dene camps along the shore, though not apparently used recently, thought Oberholtzer. At one point the two men came upon four abandoned birchbark canoes in perfect condition but left behind. This, proffered Magee, was in accordance with what he thought the Dene custom would be when one of their party had died. On August 15, the river delivered them into a large expanse of lake, the trees thinned out dramatically on the land stretching out before them, and Oberholtzer "began to think [they] had reached Nueltin Lake" and "was afraid [they] were on the edge of the Barren Lands."

⌣　⌣　⌣　⌣　⌣

The other American adventurer to pass this way in the early days of recreational canoeing, before bush planes opened up the north country, P. G. Downes—perhaps the most significant difference between the two, both Harvard graduates, is that Downes, arguably more famous, wrote about his 1939 experiences, whereas Oberholtzer did not publish an account of his trip—shared a similar concern for the rapids on this stretch of the river. Accepted canoeing techniques were different then, as Downes explained in his account of the fearsome rapids.

> You are always conscious that if the canoe strikes a ledge or is swamped and overturned, everything is lost, if not immediately, then in a longer and more hideous fashion, for with the outfit gone, there is no escape but the end of the starvation trail. . . . Always and constantly you try to follow the slick, oil-like thread of the deep water. The beauties of artistic and rhythmic paddling are forgotten. You claw and paddle with all your strength, in any fashion, manner, or method you can command at the moment. If possible, the canoe is kept moving faster than the current and so you paddle madly down the rapid to keep steerage way.

Downes—a Latin and history teacher at a school near Boston, who had taken to spending his summers traveling in northern Canada—set off from the north end of Reindeer Lake on July 6, easily three weeks ahead of Oberholtzer's schedule and without the intention to go right out to Hudson Bay. His companion on the trip was John Albrecht, who had come to Canada after the First World War, during which he fought in the German army, until captured at Ypres. From a British POW camp, he eventually found his way to Canada and became a trapper near Wollaston Lake. He was known locally to be "a good and tough traveler" as well as "a seasoned and experienced man in the North," although he was unfamiliar with this particular route north to the barrenlands. He was also an experienced canoeist with a remarkable skill in the use of a pole for both ascending and descending rapids. Downes too was not uninitiated as a northern traveler and was certainly a capable paddler. By his own account, in his wide-ranging travels he had eaten whitefish "from Reindeer Lake, Great Slave, Great Bear, salmon in Labrador, Arctic trout from Boothia peninsula and Baffin Island." He doesn't include his time on Ellesmere Island in the list—perhaps he caught no fish there.

Like Oberholtzer twenty-seven years before them, this pair had only the maps from J. B. Tyrrell and a "crude sketch map" derived from local contacts in Lac du Brochet. They had some difficulty finding the portage out of the Cochrane River into the chain of small lakes heading north. Once in those lakes, they were again in fear of losing their way and briefly contemplated turning back. At one point early in their trip, they met the old chief Casimir, in the last year of his life and, while in that camp, received some added advice on the route to the barrenlands. Downes was evidently impressed with Casimir. "Old as he was, everything about him spoke power. He was short, with a very broad back and deep chest. His face was wide and the lower jaw square and unusually heavy. There was a massiveness about him that none of the rest possessed."

Fort Hall, the trading post at the north end of Thanout (now

Fort Hall) Lake, was abandoned by the time Downes passed this site near the headwaters of the Thlewiaza. Herbert Hall had moved farther north to serve the HBC at its newer posts along the west coast of Hudson Bay, where his career as a company man was even more remarkable. In 1939, Downes described the post as "crumbling to ruin" and commented that "there is something tragic and forlorn about old abandoned trading posts." Behind Fort Hall's "bent and staggering buildings," Downes observed a cluster of eleven graves, the crosses toppled over. One noteworthy feature of the time span between Oberholtzer and Downes is the establishment and passing of numerous trading posts in the country surrounding their route.

Shortly after leaving Kasmere Lake, not far downstream from where Oberholtzer met Null-geh Josay U-gwan-i, Downes described an esker that evidently had served as a caribou trail for millennia, leading the migratory herds to their river crossing and, on many occasions in the past, providing Dene hunters with a reliable supply of meat. Behind their camp, again, he noticed a graveyard, this time with twenty-five burial sites, each with "a handmade rickety cross," all enclosed by a rough picket fence in the Dene style. To the north, beside this esker, lay a small chain of lakes that had acquired significance in the passage of time since Oberholtzer's day. The white traders had learned from the Dene that they could follow this lake-hopping route north to Putahow Lake (Cree for "I missed it"), thereby avoiding the tortuous rapids of the upcoming stretch of the Thlewiaza, and down to Nueltin Lake. It was on Putahow that Herbert Hall had established the Canoe Limit post just a few years before Oberholtzer's trip, a post that the HBC continued to operate into the 1920s. Even as Downes paused atop this esker in 1939 to look north, there still lived at Putahow one of the most eccentric independent trappers, a man called "Eskimo Charlie" Planinshek, a Yugoslav, then in his fifties, who died just five years later. From the days of Herbert Hall through the era of Eskimo Charlie—and then for some years later when names like Fred Schweder and Ragnar Jonsson were featured in the annals of this trappers' country—this region has been best known for its colorful cast of characters. Oberholtzer was here before all of that. Downes canoed here partly because of it, attracted by the romance and the storied nature of the landscape.

Downes and Albrecht arrived at Nueltin on July 24, still comfortably three weeks ahead of Oberholtzer's schedule. At the rapids where the Thlewiaza tumbles into Nueltin, he observed the centuries-old signs of Dene hunting activity at a river crossing that until recently had been the scene of the annual fall hunt. Navigation through Nueltin, which is a vast lake at least one hundred miles in length at its extremes, is by Downes' account "very confusing and a little discouraging" with "islands, bays, channels, islands everywhere . . . all one endless confusion." Nevertheless, the two men found their way to the mouth of the tributary river flowing down from Putahow—the termination of the alternate route that Downes had seen heading north beside the esker some distance upriver, before all the rapids—where they came upon a Dene camp.

⌄ ⌄ ⌄ ⌄ ⌄

Guided by two Dene men from the lone camp on the shores of Nueltin, Downes was able to follow the portage route from Nueltin to Windy Lake, farther into the barrenlands to the north. This was his true destination, where he really wanted to reach on this summer adventure. Much earlier in the trip, while visiting the camp of the old chief Casimir, Downes had been told that "the best track to Windy Lake and the Hudson's Bay post was not along the shore of Nueltin [to the mouth of Windy River], where one was very likely to be wind-bound, but to portage over and pass through a series of small lakes to the west of Nueltin just before the main narrows of the lake." Without the strong paddling of his two new partners, and their knowledge of the land, this short but difficult leg of the trip would probably not have been accomplished.

As the heavily burdened canoe—loaded with four paddlers,

their gear, plus the spoils of a successful caribou hunt on the shores of Windy Lake—reached the end of the lake and felt the tug of the current where Windy River flows out (headed back down to Nueltin Lake, farther east), dusk was upon the party. Nonetheless, they pushed on, bumping and grinding their way, rather dangerously, down the river. It became even darker. Still they pushed on until "across the river [they] could barely see, ghostly and silent, the outlines of two small shacks and the dim forms of two tents on the shore." As they approached the tiny post, they heard voices. Then, as the bow of the canoe neared the beach, one of the Dene men leaned over to Downes and whispered, "T'enna!" (Eskimos).

The three Inuit men had come to the HBC post to trade, traveling overland from their camp on the banks of the Kazan River. The trader reported that the Inuit had suffered a difficult winter, losing six members of their camp to starvation. This post, though situated on the margin where it could serve both Dene and Inuit, did most of its trade with the inland Inuit. The Dene, it seems, preferred to endure the long return journey south to Brochet. In any case, the Dene now came this far north mainly in search of caribou. The trader, Fred Schweder, who had been in the North for thirty years, had been here at Windy River for several years. He had not seen another non-Native since a one-man patrol of the RCMP had passed through in midwinter. He had received no news from outside for seven months. He welcomed Downes and Albrecht into the post and, even though it was now well past midnight, sat the two hungry men down to a welcome meal, and a long conversation.

It could be said that this lonely outpost was the only place in the world where the Inuit, the Dene, the white men, and the Cree all came together, the latter as freighters delivering goods north from Reindeer Lake. It must have been a remarkable scene at times.

It was not yet the end of July, and Downes had reached his destination, the post at Windy Lake, where he wished to linger, the better to fully enjoy the experience. He had to resolve this with the conflicting desires of his partner, John Albrecht, and the two Dene men who had left their camp on Nueltin in order to show these strangers the way. None of the three wished to linger. Albrecht felt the pressure of a long return journey by canoe to Brochet. The two Dene knew the caribou would soon be descending from the north, compelling them to prepare for the most important hunt of the year—they must return to their family's camp without further hesitation.

On August 1, the three set off in the canoe, leaving Downes behind at the post. Though uncertain of his egress, he could not bear to leave so soon, having finally achieved his long-held ambition to be there. "At last I had found what I wanted," he wrote. "Here I was free, here there was no time, here was a world which to myself I could call my own for just a little while for no one could get to it unless they had the desire that had been mine." He hoped to have time to enjoy the surroundings, perhaps to see firsthand the great caribou migration and in the end to hitch a ride out on the HBC supply plane that Schweder felt sure must come eventually, for his shelves were bare. Not even a shred of tobacco was left, the one thing that every trading post across the North made sure it was never without. The gamble paid off rather sooner than expected. On August 6, Downes left in a Canadian Airways Junkers floatplane bound for Churchill and adventures beyond.

⌣   ⌣   ⌣   ⌣   ⌣

Oberholtzer, for his part, did not meet anyone on the shores of Nueltin Lake. In contrast, his experience of the lake included abandoned Dene camps, thunderstorms, hot days, changeable weather, cold rains, and above all, navigational confusion.

▷ ▷ *While we sat round the fire waiting for the rain, we both came to the conclusion that perhaps we were going back down the lake where we had come from by a different route; we thought we had better go back first and search the north shore.*

As they paddled back and forth, often retracing their steps, so to speak, after finding themselves deep in a dead-end bay, there was evident cause for frustration. They had no map to speak of and the lake was indeed a "maze of stony bays and islands," as Oberholtzer described it—so none of this experience presented any real surprise. On occasions, when the conditions were inclement, the two men stayed put, relaxing in their tent and avoiding the cold, wet weather. It dawned on Oberholtzer, two days and very few miles into Nueltin, that this could prove troublesome.

▷ ▷ *I was sorry I had not travelled all day. I began to realize what an expense it would mean to me to arrive at Churchill much after September 1st, and made preparation for a very early start in the morning.*

This he wrote before bed on August 17. Realistically, their chances of making it to Churchill by September 1 had already evaporated. It was the risk not to his pocketbook but rather to their lives that this simple fact implied, which apparently remained lost to Oberholtzer.

On August 22, after a week in Nueltin, they were not yet halfway down the lake's one-hundred-mile length. But the route ahead did clarify at this point, at the major narrows dividing the lake in two, when they climbed a high hill in order to survey the route.

▷ ▷ *After dinner we paddled another five miles up the bay to the foot of a very high, conspicuous ridge. It runs southwest and northeast parallel to the water and rises gradually in an even slope from both ends. We began to climb it at five o'clock and were well repaid. The contour for miles around looked like a great relief map. Far on the east, north, and west were high hills or ridges. Long narrow bays extend south. The islands everywhere resemble the lake in shape, narrow necks connecting larger bodies, sort of figure eights. Magnificent view. Hill probably five hundred feet high. Easy to climb, two or three small muskegs between the different levels;*

strange rostrum-like level places of gravel two or three feet in diameter all the way up. At sunset on a rock at the very top I left a can, in which was a page out of my [note] book. It gave the date and condition of our supplies and said that we had named the hill "Hawkes Summit" in honor of Mr. Arthur Hawkes.

Leaving the narrows behind, they struck out to the northeast, into a lake that appeared to go on forever. They paddled across the open expanse of the mouth of Hearne Bay where 142 years before them Samuel Hearne had crossed during his unfathomable, inimitable journey to the Arctic Ocean, the same feat that had so inspired Oberholtzer during his early reading about northern explorations. He was the first white man to see·this lake, and before Oberholtzer, there had been very few since. Even with the advantage of having seen the way ahead, the two men repeatedly found themselves in dead-end bays as they struggled to find the river's exit from Nueltin. The going was very tough at times—no more barefoot portaging now.

▷ ▷ *At daybreak there was a slight drizzle. We got up at half past three by my watch and, though I had had a restless night, I felt better. The morning was still cloudy but not cold. I put on woollen under-drawers. We traveled north along the east shore for an hour till we found we were in a bay from which it was necessary to paddle several miles west between a narrow shallow opening to reach the main lake. The lake looked very dreary, monotonous wavy ridges on both sides, heavy, thick, wet clouds overhead, and only a streak of saffron and green in the east where the sun was struggling to get through. Every time we had a shower of drizzle it felt cold. Our course lay north-east another hour's paddle until we came to an opening in the east. As the lake did not appear to extend much farther north we felt obliged to explore this bay.*

It, too, led nowhere, and they once again retraced their steps. This pattern was repeated over and over again. One can only imagine how frustrating it must have felt. On August 28, now thirteen days since they had entered this long lake at its southern extremity, Oberholtzer recorded that "somehow [they] had the feeling that [they] were near the river." That feeling followed closely on what must have been, for both men, an extraordinary experience.

▷ ▷ *The sun came out hot for a few minutes, and we went on down into the bay to investigate. We heard a very big fish flop right behind the canoe and Billy said it must be some new kind he did not know. Not even a sturgeon would jump behind the canoe. The next minute he was calling for the gun. Right behind us was a black head, which kept following us about. It was a seal. I had hard work to persuade Billy not to shoot him. Luckily one shot missed. The animal followed us for half an hour, while we looked into three or four very stony bays.*

One might assume, of course, that if there were seals about, it could not be far to the sea. What did Oberholtzer think? He didn't say. But the encouraging—though in this case misleading—thought must have crossed his mind. Nevertheless, the end of Nueltin was nigh.

▷ ▷ *The ridges looked as if they were on the brink; all the land to the east seemed lower. Yet there was no large opening. Finally, as we were approaching the most northerly of the several small indentures, I noticed that the weeds were pointing the same way. Then I got out on the point and saw that the water did extend half a mile farther at least and there the next moment, having passed through a very narrow but deep channel, we noticed a slight current, which became stronger at the next narrows and brought us to the head of a rapid.*

They had, at last, reached the Thlewiaza's outlet from Nueltin Lake. It was midday on August 28. Oberholtzer's desire to reach Churchill by September 1 had vanished, though he made no further reference to this schedule. An unknown stretch of river lay ahead, to be followed by the even more daunting uncertainty of a passage across Hudson Bay. Some unspoken concern must have been brewing in his mind.

◁ ▷   ◁ ▷   ◁ ▷   ◁ ▷   ◁ ▷   ◁ ▷   ◁ ▷   ◁ ▷   ◁ ▷

A Modern Paddler's Perspective

Down the Thlewiaza to Nueltin Lake

The country begins to change slightly past the narrows where Chief Casimir is buried. Weeds bending downstream in the narrows where Fort Hall Lake gives way to Thanout Lake remind a paddler that this *is* a river.

From Thanout Lake, the Thlewiaza narrows as it meanders between steep sandy shores for about seven kilometers to the head of Kasmere Falls. Here the tranquil, easy mood of the river suddenly vanishes. As if to proclaim that the Thlewiaza is a real river, Kasmere Falls chases a twisted, tortuous route

The Thlewiaza near where it enters Nueltin Lake.

through scoured rock for more than a mile, dropping dramatically into Kasmere Lake. About a mile long, the portage past Kasmere Falls starts at a small pond on the north shore of the river and winds through sand, rock, and wet ground. This marks the first hint at hard portaging—there is much worse to come. The soft, sandy hills start to give way to bald bedrock. You can still find sand beaches and flat campsites, but now you have to search them out.

A few miles downstream from Kasmere Lake, the Thlewiaza cuts through a sand esker and makes a sharp turn to the south. This long esker winds its way south from Putahow Lake, its top deeply rutted with an ancient caribou trail that leads from Putahow to this crossing of the Thlewiaza River and beyond. On the south side of the river a trail climbs up the esker, and at the top lies a Dene site with a dozen graves surrounded by hand-hewn picket fences and crosses. Although the surrounding area is largely burned, the fire wrapped around these graves and left them untouched.

Rock defines the rapid descent from Kasmere Lake to Nueltin Lake. The rapids start in earnest after Kasmere; most are narrow and chase through glacier-scoured channels studded with canoe-eating rocks. Shorelines are deep right to shore, most often covered in dense alder and willow. Birch and white spruce tip over the river, and tamarack are not uncommon. Lining over moss-covered rocks or walking along the shore through the dense forest is often all but impossible. Even today's highly skilled paddlers, with nearly indestructible boats, will find themselves lining and portaging many times from Kasmere to Nueltin. Earlier travelers, in their birch-bark or cedar canoes, had to be much more careful and portage more often.

Casting a small spoon or fly into the fast current of one of these rapids quickly becomes a lesson in the Dene language. As soon as your hook crosses the eddy line, you are almost certain to watch an Arctic grayling hit and then dance high out of the water. The name of this river literally translated means "little fish"—it is likely these fish that gave the river its name.

On a map of Canada's ecozones, the entire length of Nueltin is within the Taiga Shield. Without having been there, you might think that it would be much the same from south to north—perhaps like paddling the length of Reindeer Lake where the sounds and scenery and smells stay largely the same. According to the maps, after all, the South Arctic Ecozone still lies far to the north.

Knowing that the people of "the land of little sticks," the Dene, felt more comfortable on the southern half of this lake, while the people of the barrenlands, the Caribou Inuit, preferred to camp on the northern half, helps to paint a different picture.

Nueltin runs directly south to north. As you paddle north on the Lake of the Sleeping Island it is like walking up a mountain. The land quickly changes from soft, sandy, well-treed parkland to harsh, rock-studded, treeless barren lands. Each new campsite leaves you wondering how any landscape can change so quickly.

At the south end of Nueltin Lake, the gentler landform seems to wrap around you and offer protection and comfort. It feels safe. No matter how bad a storm, or how violent a wind, you know that you can huddle into the rolling sand hills, sheltered by a copse of trees while you sip tea and warm your hands over a fire made from a limitless supply of firewood. Yet simply walking to the top of one of the hills that protect you will offer a hint at what is to come as you head north. Largely bare of trees, the higher ground is a mat of miniature Labrador tea, juniper, cranberries, and bearberry. Country like this looks inviting on a warm, windless day, but the thought of camping here in a storm quickly makes you appreciate your camp safely nestled in the pocket of spruce below. The view from these hilltops extends forever until it dissolves into the hazy horizon of soft grays and mauves. Not everyone who sees this limitless landscape feels comfortable. To some it is simply too big, too overwhelming, too bare, and too fraught with possible danger. But for those who are drawn to it, there is no cure but to go farther and farther. The forests of the south quickly lose much of their mystery and remoteness. They become the country you have to travel through to get to the land of little sticks and beyond to the tundra.

Nueltin is a land of extremes. Where else can hot unrelenting sun force you into the lake at lunch just to cool off one day, only to find the next you're searching for winter mitts and down jacket as you watch violent gray clouds, borne by unrelenting winds, race toward your camp. One day you paddle across a lake under cloudless blue skies, the water so calm it feels as if you are somehow stuck and your canoe won't move no matter how hard you paddle. The next, you could be fighting cold headwinds or surfing on the tops of huge waves. It is a land of dramatic change. Everything about this country speaks in superlatives. From freezing cold to scorching hot to insects by the millions to the bluest blues and greenest greens to the most dramatic alpine scenery and the longest, most sinuous eskers imaginable, there is no subtlety here. It is a land that touches you and whispers magic in your ear.

A little more than a hundred years ago, a missionary met a Chipewyan man on the edge of the barrenlands in this same transition zone where Nueltin lies. Saltatha knew this land well. He had traveled widely, all his life, in a never-ending search for caribou. His people depended on the caribou for their every need, from food to clothing and shelter. The missionary, no doubt a devout and well-intentioned man, was a stranger to this land, at the very edge of white men's sphere of knowledge. He was there for a reason, and he proceeded to tell Saltatha of the peace and beauty that awaited them in heaven. Saltatha listened carefully. When the missionary finished, Saltatha spoke: "My father, you have spoken well. You have told me that heaven is very beautiful. Tell me now one thing more. Is it more beautiful than the country of the musk ox in summer, when sometimes the mist blows over the lakes, and sometimes the water is blue, and the loons cry very often?"

Dene Reflections

This country, at the transition from boreal forest to tundra, seen in the larger historical perspective, is predominantly Dene territory. The oral history of these proud people reflects their attachment to the land and to this northern country in particular, though today they live farther south. In former times, their annual peregrinations found them walking over this country in search of caribou. They followed the caribou. In this manner, they survived for centuries, even millennia, before the white man arrived, before the Inuit moved inland from the coast. This area was indisputably part of the Dene homeland. Their oral history tells the tale.

ALFRED DENECHEZHE
b. 1918
Lac Brochet, 2005

I was about six when my mother died. From then on, my father brought me up. In those days, we didn't have much supplies. Out on the tundra, traveling with my Dad, we had an old frying pan. We used to cut up meat and boil it in that pan. That's how we survived.

We were really poor. Dad used to make me moccasins and caribou clothing. We were living in Windy Lake. One time after the caribou went south, there was nothing to eat, so everyone left. We went to the north end of Nueltin Lake, out in the barrenlands. One time, my uncle's tent got completely drifted over with snow there, and he had to cut his way out of the top of the tent, using a knife.

Everyone else moved down south to where the caribou were, south of sixty. My Dad and I were the only ones left. We went to the post at Windy Lake. The people there helped. So we went back north to Thlewiaza and found a patch of tamarack. We camped there, put our tent up, and used the wood for fire. We trapped from there.

A group of Dene from the group now in Tadoule Lake arrived with four toboggans and dogs. So we all stayed together. Those other Dene knew the country well. It was more their traditional territory. They said there were more trees closer to the coast and some caribou there too. So we all moved east, downriver.

After a while, the other Dene wanted to leave (probably to go get some supplies or trade some fur), so they all but one left. We arranged to meet back at the first patch of tamarack in two weeks' time. When they came back, they brought lots of stuff, including

a box of candy for me. The trapping was good, mostly for white fox. After that the group stayed together there the rest of the winter. Those other Dene were from Two Rivers Lake, down by Churchill, and they went back there, a long trip.

After that, my Dad and I moved back to Windy Lake, briefly. I remember making a sled with two tamaracks and a caribou skin, loading it with tent and stove and pulling it with just two dogs.

Later, as a young man, I had just four dogs, and I was trapping on my own. I traveled long distances and still remember lots of those places. We had Dene names for every lake and river.

Alfred Denechezhe,
Lac Brochet, 2005.

All that area around Nueltin was used by Dene. When the caribou were there, lots of Dene. Then we'd follow the caribou south. But some Dene stayed on the barrenlands all year round. Mostly the only white man's food they wanted was tea and tobacco—for all their food they got it from the land. It used to be amazing, in those days, people would come all the way to Brochet to get supplies, mostly tea. The tobacco was different—once it was gone, that was okay. But if they ran out of tea, they had to go to the HBC.

The boundary of the provinces (Manitoba and Saskatchewan) should've been the treeline, instead of sixty [degrees North].

Casimir used to take me to Brochet by dog team. He's my grandfather. Helen was my mother. He was a small man. But he was really stubborn. He wouldn't change his mind. He had to have his way. He became the chief when they signed the treaty, selected by the people, because he was able to lead. He knew how to survive. At that treaty signing, when government offered money, he didn't want to accept it. He said it would bring problems in the future.

There's a rock in Brochet where the treaty was signed. The Indian agent said that government would help the Dene so long as that rock exists and the sun rises. Well that rock is still there.

The second year of the treaty [actually, several years later], when Casimir met the Indian agent, he told him they wanted him to bring canoes. The next year, when he showed up with no canoes for the Dene, Casimir refused to accept the treaty money, saying they wouldn't take the money until and unless the government sent canoes. The government solved the dilemma, eventually, by giving the money to Romi [Samuel] and making him the chief. That was the end of Casimir's time as chief.

The Brochet Reserve was originally Dene but is now taken over by the Crees. That was Dene land. Those Cree, originally from Pelican Narrows, came up on freighters bringing goods up to Brochet [for HBC, etc.]. That's how they first became interrelated with the Dene in Brochet.

With all the disturbance of caribou north of sixty*—tourist camps, airstrips, mineral exploration—it's amazing we still get caribou down here in winter. All that development happened on Dene land without anyone consulting with us.

Dene ended up in Brochet by following the caribou. They started up around Nueltin Lake and just followed the caribou south for the winter, ending up around Brochet.

The Creator gave Dene caribou for our survival.

---

* The sixtieth parallel (60°N) is the boundary across the top of Canada's western provinces: Manitoba, Saskatchewan, and Alberta. "North of sixty" are the Northwest Territories and Nunavut.

LEON DENECHEZHE
b. 1937
Lac Brochet, 2005

I lived around Kasmere Lake as a youngster. My grandfather is buried there in the graveyard, with some other family members—a lot of people died of sickness there.

The earliest I remember is traveling all over with my Dad up to Nueltin and Ennadai and Poorfish lakes. We used to leave the families within the treeline, for shelter, and the men went up onto the barrenlands to trap white fox. There was big demand at that time.

So much has changed since I was young. My parents just moved to where they could survive, on the land. Even the environment has changed—the weather, migration routes and habits of the wildlife. In the old days, people lived where they could survive, mostly on caribou and fish. Now, in the modern community, we seem to be contained within a boundary.

Leon Denechezhe,
Lac Brochet, 2005.

Those trips out onto the barrenlands, the best time for foxes was November to January, but in February it seemed harder to catch them. Every winter, we'd meet up with Inuit there. We traded dogs, harnesses, caribou clothing, lots of things.

I came back from school (just one year) at Sturgeon at age fifteen. At sixteen I traveled with my Dad trapping. Starting at seventeen, I traveled on my own.

In 1988, I built a cabin at Poorfish Lake. Ninety-four was my last year of trapping there, traveling up from Lac Brochet. Some years were better for foxes than others. It depended on the sea, the ice on Hudson Bay—most of the foxes went out onto the ice, but if the ice comes right to shore, there are lots of fox on the land.

One time near Putahow Lake, on the way home, I caught thirty foxes just overnight.

My Dad used to tell me stories about my grandfather. He didn't trap foxes. He went after marten, using traditional deadfall traps. He traveled by foot on snowshoe, pulling a small sled, and would set one hundred traps. In those days, before the fox trade, Dene stayed mostly within the treeline during winter. Same for us, when I was sixteen, seventeen, etc. After February, we'd move back within the trees and trap marten, muskrat, lynx for the rest of the winter.

I used to work hauling freight from Brochet to Windy Lake, three hundred pounds of freight, paddling a nineteen-foot canoe, two men to a canoe. We were paid one hundred dollars a trip and made three trips in a summer.

Redhead was famous for his dog team and for being a man who never quits. If he found a track of an animal, he'd follow it and never turn back until he found it. He was Dene, but he had a special gift. An old lady who knew him told me a story of a time when Redhead saw tracks of reindeer. He followed them for three nights, and every time he got close, they ran away. One time, on the third day, he saw them lying down at the edge of a lake with a bare hill behind them. Instead of going across the lake, he went right around the lake and used the hill to hide himself as he approached. He killed all seven of them. Reindeer are bigger and have different coloring on their face. They still come around here, with caribou. Redhead was a demanding and determined person. One time, he traveled from Brochet to Fort Hall by dog team in one day.

JIMMY DZEYLION
b. 1917 (now deceased)

I have trapped many miles away, where there are no trees, in the barrenlands. The lake is called Kasba Lake. I stayed at the edge of the treeline. It's barren just a few feet from where I stayed. There are trees in some places, but mostly it's just barren land. There are many white fox. I trapped white fox for three years using a dog team. I used seven dogs. There were no Ski Doos. Sometimes I could not find firewood. I got very hungry at times. There are snow banks as high as a house. I lived inside a snow bank with my dogs when I was trapping, but this was not a good living because it got really cold.

We dressed like Eskimos then. There were no white man's parkas. All the clothing we wore was made of caribou. One time, on December 23, I came back from trapping to Brochet. I had over one hundred white fox pelts. I made lots of money.

ELY SAMUEL
b. 1939
Brochet, 2005

I still go trapping north of Kasmere Lake along Putahow River and to Poorfish Lake and beyond. I had a cabin just southwest of Poorfish Lake. I sometimes went farther north trapping to Ennadai and right up to Whitefish Lake. I first went up to the Nueltin Lake area with my father when I was about twenty-two, and I kept going every year until about 2000. The first three years was by dog team. It took five or six days from Brochet to get to that cabin. After that, by an old Ski Doo, it took two days. I went up in late October, stayed until Christmas, and then came back down to Brochet. I was trapping fox, lynx, marten, anything. My best year ever was ninety white fox. Usually I got twenty to thirty marten and lynx. I went close to where the Inuit were, but I've never met any of them up there.

Ely Samuel, Brochet, 2005.

HELENISE BESSKKAYSTARE
b. 1923
Wollaston, 2005

I was born at Nueltin Lake. I had eight brothers and sisters. They are all dead now. When my father was still alive, we stayed around Nueltin Lake. That's where I grew up. Most of the time we stayed there.

Before Christmas people used to travel to Brochet. The men went and the women stayed behind to look after the children and do some fishing. The men were usually gone about two weeks. Then when the ice melted, the men would go again, by canoe. They'd be gone as long as two months.

There was two places where there was a little store, closer, somewhere around Nueltin. I remember people took their furs there to trade for groceries. There was no money, just little sticks for trading. They went for flour, sugar, tea, bacon, tobacco, bullets. All the goods for those Nueltin posts were carried up there from Brochet by Dene and Cree, by dog team in winter and canoe in summer.

Helenise Besskkaystare, Wollaston, 2005.

Those two little trading posts were also used by Inuit. I played with Inuit children in Nueltin. They were friendly. The elders used to say, "Don't go near them, they're bad people." I was happy when they came. North of Nueltin, there used to be Inuit camped.

I miss those places a lot, but I'll probably never go back there.

Trappers' Country

What a different place this whole region would have seemed just ten years after Oberholtzer canoed through the southern fringe of the barrenlands in 1912. Following the end of the First World War, the price of fur rose dramatically. Men from far and wide looked north for new excitement and a way to make their dreams of unfound riches come true: Americans, Swedes, Germans, Norwegians, Danes, and strangely, only very few Canadians.

By contrast, when P. G. Downes arrived in Churchill (by floatplane!) at the end of his trip in 1939, he stayed with a pair of trappers from the Nueltin Lake area, Windy Smith and Jerry Kemp. They are but two of a long list of names that make up the honor roll of those who trapped in the Nueltin Lake country. By the late 1920s, the country surrounding Nueltin Lake was fairly crawling with white men seeking their fortune, or at least their financial independence: Del Simons, Dick Halcrow, Syd Keighley, Wallace Laird, George Yandle, Jim Ingram, Alfred Peterson, Frits Oftedal, Bill Mackenzie, Jack Lundie, Dave Lundy (the two Lundies are probably brothers—some of the spellings used by trappers were at times erratic), Cecil "Husky" Harris, George Lush, Albert "Frenchy" Tremblay, Karl and Bill Bucholtz—it's a lengthy list. One of these men, Husky Harris, was able to tell Downes about his sole predecessor as a "recreational" paddler on the route from Reindeer Lake to Nueltin, following the old way north, a man named "Oberhauser, or Obenhauser," as he told it. Harris knew this because, in 1924, he had discovered Oberholtzer's note in a can on top of Hawkes Summit beside Nueltin Lake.

The intervening years, between Oberholtzer and Downes, saw the ascendance of the white-fox fur trade, the era of the independent trapper. In the early days the trappers paddled north from

Reindeer Lake, following the old way north, with their canoes loaded down by a winter's worth of supplies. They were solitary men, to an extreme. The trapper, alone or with a single partner, assembled his outfit. Every item was essential, nothing surplus; everything had to be carried. The lot—traps, staple foods, pots and pans, tents, rifles, ammunition, fishnets, dog harness, sled, and dogs—was loaded into a canoe. The trapper pushed his canoe off from the shore in front of the Lac du Brochet post and headed north, bound for the edge of the barrenlands, or as the trappers said, "the Country."

To survive, the trapper needed to find two things: caribou and wood. The strategy was straightforward enough but far from simple: find a wooded patch sufficient to build a log cabin and cut enough firewood to last the winter, and be ready when the caribou migration came through sometime in late summer. With only an axe, a bag of spikes, and a lot of muscle, the trapper would fell and strip the trees, move them into place one atop the other, stuff moss into the cracks, and in no more than two weeks have his cabin ready.

Next came the quest for food. There was not only himself to feed but the dogs too—dogs upon whom he would need to depend for his life during the coming winter. If the caribou were not yet in the area, then fishnets were set and tended daily. The fish could be hung and dried, ready as dog food for the long winter months. Fishing was much easier now, with open water or even with early winter's thin ice, than it would be later when the ice would grow to several feet thick.

But nothing was more important than the caribou. The trappers were fond of quoting the Indians: "The caribou are like ghosts; they come from nowhere, fill up all the land, then disappear." When they came, the trapper worked hard to put up a store of meat. That done, he was ready for winter and the main purpose of his trip: trapping the elusive white fox. By then the barrenlands were snow covered, and the lakes were frozen; sled travel was once again possible.

By the time the snow fell in earnest and stayed, everything was ready. The sled was loaded, the traces laid out, and each harness checked. The dogs, tethered individually along a chain stretched between two trees or stakes, knew immediately what was happening. They strained at their anchors, eager to be on the trail, for there was nothing a dog loved more than to please his master. One barrenlands trapper, Gus D'Aoust, described his dogs and their relationship.

> I had a lot of respect for my dogs and they had respect for me in return. I would talk to my dogs just as if I was talking to a human, and they would look at me, listen, and wag their tails. They understood me. I treated them well, and they came first. It's true that a man's best friend is his dog. They worked their hearts out for me. I could always depend on them and they would never abandon me if I was in trouble. I put my trust in them.

There were trappers and traders, and sometimes the line between them blurred. There were company men (traders with the Hudson's Bay Company or Revillon Frères) and independents, the latter basically trappers who saw an advantage to having others do their trapping for them, with the intent—as did most of the independent trappers—of shipping out the fur themselves for sale in the markets to the south. Not infrequently, men who worked for one company became independent traders for a while or changed allegiance altogether and worked for another company. A third category of entrepreneur in the Country was the tripper, who was paid to go traveling out to the camps, both Dene and Inuit, and trade on behalf of someone else; these men might, of course, do a little trapping themselves on the side. There was more than a little confusion, and although the men involved were all essentially competing for the same resource, often representing companies that were bitter rivals, as individuals they were inclined to cooperate with each other, travel together, and not infrequently save each others' lives. That was the way of the North.

Even before the mania for white fox fur, Herbert Hall, working

for the Hudson's Bay Company, had pushed the trade north between 1906 and 1908 by establishing new posts in the region.
That was arguably the beginning of the effective pursuit of the
trade with the inland Inuit in their own land. Trade for the first
few years was relatively slow. That changed after the First World
War. Suddenly, fox fur was in fashion. The rush into fur country
happened swiftly. In 1922, Adolphe Lapensée opened his post at
Sandy Hills beside the Cochrane River. That same year, Revillon
Frères opened a post at the mouth of the Putahow River on Nueltin
Lake. In 1924, the Hudson's Bay Company opened a post at Poorfish Lake, just west of Nueltin. Then came the individuals: independent traders, trappers, and trippers. It was almost as good as
the lure of gold in Alaska and Yukon. A single pelt was worth
twenty-five to thirty dollars,* and over the next ten years that
price doubled. A really good trapper might get five hundred pelts
in a winter season.

Syd Keighley's story offers a fair illustration of the life. For a
year, over the winter of 1927 to 1928, he took a sabbatical from the
HBC in order to try his hand at trapping independently. He and a
partner, Frenchy Tremblay, lived with their families in an old
shack, built by George Yandle some years earlier, beside Putahow
Lake, just west of Nueltin. Keighley remarked that it was a busy
place.

> For such an isolated part of the country, there was no shortage
> of neighbours. Dick Halcrow, who was trapping south of me,
> came up and ran a trapline in the vicinity so we traveled a lot
> together. George Yandle, who was living with his Eskimo wife,
> trapped and ran a Revillon Frères outpost at the north end of
> Nueltin Lake. Alfred Peterson, running a post for Del Simons,
> was near George at Windy Lake. Just north of them I had
> my Red River outpost, and a few miles downstream was Karl
> Bucholtz, in charge of a Revillon Frères post. With Karl was his
> brother, Bill, who was spending his first winter in the north.

* In 1925, Cdn$30 would have been equivalent to Cdn$364 in 2007. Sell-
ing five hundred pelts at this price would have netted the equivalent of
Cdn$182,000 today.

Another neighbour was Bill McKenzie, an old Scotsman from the Orkneys, who had crossed the Atlantic in a sailing ship and landed at Churchill sometime in the 1860s when he was sixteen years old. He trapped near the south end of Ennadai Lake.

When Keighley and Tremblay first arrived, they met three Inuit men who had come down to trade with Jack Lundie. Lundie was on Putahow that year also, at the old HBC post at the northwestern extremity of the lake, with four freighter canoes full of trading goods he had brought from Reindeer Lake during the summer. His plan was to move this mountain of freight overland to the north, after freeze-up, and there to trade with the Inuit. Not long after freeze-up, in late October, Keighley and Tremblay met two more Inuit men on their way to find Windy Smith at Nueltin Lake. On another trip, in midwinter, the pair of trappers ran into three more Inuit men in the middle of a frozen lake with their dog teams. "We came across three Eskimos sitting out in the middle of a small lake eating raw frozen caribou meat with no fire and no tea although there was a lot of scrub brush around the shore of the lake that they could have used both for shelter and for a fire. They preferred the open lake for their meal in spite of the extreme cold and a bitter northwest wind."

Their winter's take of fur sold the next spring for $2,300.* The next year, Tremblay and his wife stayed on trapping, while Keighley went back to work for the HBC. Together with his wife and son, he ran the post on Poorfish Lake, originally built in 1924 by Dick Halcrow (who, at different times, worked for both Revillon and the HBC). Soon after they settled in, a group of Inuit arrived, having walked over from Ennadai Lake to see whether the post was going to be open for the winter. It proved to be an active winter of trade for Keighley with the Inuit of Ennadai Lake.

One of the Inuit who came regularly to trade from the Kazan River was named Kakoot, a man who not only was a very success-

---

* In 1928, Cdn$2,300 would have been the equivalent of Cdn$28,175 in 2007.

ful hunter and trapper but also acted as a middleman for trade with other Inuit. He became so well known to the trappers and traders around Nueltin that he was engaged to be a guide for Captain Thierry Mallet, president of the Revillon Frères, in 1926. Mallet came north to inspect the company's posts and to venture farther north by way of exploration. He was an adventurer in his own right. Del Simons, free trader, and two Cree canoemen from Cumberland House, Peter Linklater and Joe Cadotte, accompanied the expedition to the Kazan River. Guided by Kakoot, they paddled downstream, visiting Inuit camps along the way, as far as Yathkyed Lake, known aptly as Hikuligjuaq by the Inuit, meaning the Large Ice-filled One. Here, in mid-July, their way was blocked by solid ice, so they turned around to fight their way back upstream, heading south once again. Mallet was fortunate to see the caribou migration, which he called "the most stupendous sight of wild game in North America since the bygone days of the buffalo." Of Kakoot, whom he called "my friend," Mallet wrote at length in the *Atlantic Monthly.*

> Kakoot is by far the most intelligent and the most prosperous Eskimo among the thirty-odd families which form the entire population of that part of the Barren Lands [the Kazan valley]. He knows three hundred miles of the western shores of Hudson Bay, has been as far as Boothia to the north and the Great Slave Lake to the west, and has picked up a lot of knowledge and experience through dealing with other tribes and meeting, occasionally, white men.
>
> He relies, of course, on his own hunt, meat and fur, to obtain all the necessities of life. Nevertheless he is a born trader and does not hesitate to journey south to the trees so as to get a small outfit of goods which enables him to collect part of the other Eskimos' white foxes. His igloo and topek [*tupik*, or "tent"] contain priceless treasures in the eyes of the other natives.

Kakoot continued to visit the trading posts around Nueltin for at least fifteen years after this trip with Mallet—there are photographs of him outside one or more posts to prove it. He died in the

1940s. His grave, on a small island in Dimma Lake, on the Kazan River, is a grand affair by Inuit standards. He is entombed by his overturned cedar-ribbed canoe, together with at least one of his three wives and surrounded by his wealth: a brass-bound wooden trunk, an old phonograph, an alarm clock, a meat grinder, hunting equipment, and all manner of paraphernalia.

By the time Kakoot passed away, the dwindling population of Inuit in the Kazan valley—disease and starvation had taken their toll—had several options for their trade. The HBC post at Eskimo Point (now Arviat), established in 1921, had become a major center of commerce, with outposts stretching inland toward the Kazan River. Revillon Frères had been absorbed by the HBC. Most of the independent traders had either made their fortune or given up. The onset of the Second World War reduced the fashionable interest in fox fur, and by the mid-1940s, the price of fox dropped dramatically.

A few hardy white trappers remained, however. One of those was Eskimo Charlie Planinshek, of whom P. G. Downes had written. He was as much a recluse as anyone could be. He erected posts topped with human skulls about his camp in order to scare away uninvited intruders. He lived and died in a hovel on the edge of the barrenlands, with a garden of flowers and vegetables to one side. He was a small man with piercing blue eyes, typically dressed in torn and patched old clothing. Originally from Yugoslavia,* he had spent some time in Mexico—fighting alongside Pancho Villa, according to one story—before settling in Canada and wandering northward. He married a Cree woman in 1915, Jane Mary Ballendine from Pelican Narrows, with whom he had two surviving children, a daughter, Inez, and a son, Tony.† In the early 1930s, with his two children, eight and six years old, respectively, he undertook a remarkable journey by canoe. Setting out from Windy Lake in October of 1929, he paddled right down to the Gulf of

* Planinshek was from Slovenia, the northwestern-most state of the former Yugoslavia. It is now the independent country the Republic of Slovenia.
† They actually had five children, but only two survived beyond childhood.

Mexico and then back up the Atlantic coast, using the inland waterway, to New York and Montreal. Along the way, his children danced for the crowds dressed in caribou skin clothing—he told the crowds his children were part Eskimo—and Eskimo Charlie saved up the proceeds to pay for his children's education. The reclusive trapper died beside Putahow in 1947 in his midsixties. When an RCMP patrol found him in his bunk, dead some eighteen months, he was buried, and his own flowers, out of his garden, were placed on his grave.

Since the arrival of the railroad at Churchill in 1929, the Hudson Bay port and railhead had become the favored jumping-off point for trappers headed up the Thlewiaza into the country around Nueltin. Resupply of the HBC posts at Eskimo Point, others along the coast north of Churchill, and the few remaining independent posts inland was also made easier by the train. After the time Downes came through in 1939, the Schweders, whom he visited at the Windy River HBC post, moved down to the river mouth at Nueltin Lake and set up their own post. The older boys were active trappers, and Inuit from the Kazan River continued to visit them.

Their main trapline carved an eighty-mile circle west and north from Windy River to encompass Ennadai Lake. Along the way, they would stop to visit Inuit camps by the Kazan River. In early 1947, on just such a trip, a scene of devastation met twenty-two-year-old Charlie Schweder. In every camp, he found starvation and death. In one camp there remained only two small children, Anoteelik and Kukwik (later Rita), the latter only five years old. In other camps he found more survivors, all in desperate condition. He persuaded them all to follow him home, where he had meat enough for everyone. Many Inuit survived because of Charlie Schweder, and he adopted the two children as his own—they lived with Charlie and his brothers at the Windy River post.

That summer a research biologist, Francis Harper, and his young assistant, Farley Mowat, came to stay with the Schweders at Windy River in order to study the caribou. The expedition, mounted by the Arctic Institute, picked the location after reading

P. G. Downes's book *Sleeping Island,* about his 1939 trip, published in 1943. It proved to be a less than harmonious group of
people, but it nevertheless gave Mowat the material needed for his
subsequently famous books on the Caribou Inuit and the southern
barrenlands. Charlie Schweder and Farley Mowat paddled down
the Thlewiaza together, which Mowat described as "a confused
mass of boulders and jagged rocks and the water runs sometimes
only a few inches over them."

After he moved to Churchill more or less permanently in 1950,
Charlie Schweder continued to trap and work as a guide. But he
never lost his affinity for the Nueltin Lake country. "I only have
good thoughts of the old days up north, you're doggone rights!"

By the 1950s, only one trapper was left in the Nueltin Lake
country. Ragnar Jonsson, a Swede, moved into the Country in
1938, after several years somewhat farther south trapping around
Wollaston and Reindeer lakes, an area that eventually became
"too crowded" for his liking. Years before that in 1923, he had
deserted the Swedish army, escaped on a tramp steamer, and then
jumped ship in a Canadian port. For a couple of years before
he began trapping, he tried farming, fishing, wood cutting, and
working for the railway. In 1938, when he arrived at Nueltin,
there were several other trappers still active around Nueltin, but
fifteen years later, Jonsson was left with the whole place to himself,
save the few Inuit living just to the north of his traplines. People
who knew him describe him as a man of intellect, well spoken and
worldly, though someone who was entirely comfortable with only
his own company. He often went for years without making a trip
to the outside for supplies, not to mention contact with other
humans, living on meat and fish he caught himself. When he did
go to a post for supplies, he was not that interested in human contact. One time, short on flour and other necessities, he traveled by
dog team a few hundred miles to Churchill, walked into the grocery
store there, bought what he needed, went back outside, loaded up,
and headed away out of town, without really speaking to anyone.
He subscribed to *Time* magazine, collecting years' worth of back

issues at a time so he could catch up on world events. He lived there, he claimed, in order to be free. "This is the life," he explained, "no worries, taxes or traffic. I'm free to do as I like."

During the years of the fox boom, Jonsson accumulated sufficient wealth that he was subsequently able to afford supply flights, maybe once a year, which brought him macaroni, flour, beans, whisky, sugar, tea, and coffee in large quantities. He claimed he could live like a king on five hundred dollars a year. He continued to run his trapline, probably the longest any of the trappers used at three hundred miles, along which he had a number of camps, each one a small conical-shaped tipi, the easiest shape to heat according to Jonsson. It took him two or three weeks to do a round. He continued this life in a land that in effect became his and his alone after the inland Inuit had moved to Eskimo Point, and the Dene rarely ventured so far north in their caribou hunts. He persisted into his eighties, until eventually old age and failing health forced him to move south to The Pas, where he died in 1988, nearly ninety years old. It had, apparently, been a healthy life for Ragnar Jonsson,* the last of the old-time, independent trappers. His departure signalled the end of an era in the history of Nueltin Lake.

* In 1963, when Ernest Oberholtzer, nearly eighty years old, revisited Nueltin Lake, he had occasion to meet Ragnar Jonsson and thus to forge a link with the ongoing history of the region he had long ago explored.

Nu-thel-tin-tua, Qikiqtariaktuk

Nueltin. Nu-thel-tin-tua. Sleeping Island Lake, named after a pair of islands that were thought by Dene to resemble a sleeping man lying down. It lies across the transition from taiga to tundra.

There is a Dene legend that, it is believed, refers to Nueltin. Long ago, the mother of all Dene, an old woman called Nonucho, walked south with her two children in search of an escape from the desolate, ice-covered Arctic. Every time she thought she could go no further, the wolves brought her food and reassurance that she must continue south. For years she wandered across the barren-lands. Though tired, hungry, feeble, and blind, she pressed on. Her children reported sightings of caribou and musk oxen that they could hunt. The children were now grown up, but even as adults they deferred to Nonucho, who said they must move on. Finally, walking alongside a large lake, the two children told her they could see a line of green trees, the "land of little sticks," in the distance. Their mother smiled, happy in the knowledge that they had arrived, that her job was done. "Here is the home for all our people to come," she said. Within days, she was gone, but ever since, her people have known they need only lie on the ground beside this lake in order for the spirit of Mother Nonucho to make them strong, just as she continues to deliver the caribou and musk oxen to their hunt.

Helen Joseyounen, born in 1903, now deceased, was born at Nueltin Lake and was among the last of the Dene to grow up on the edge of the barrenlands. With her first husband, she lived at Kasba Lake, the headwaters of the Kazan River, in the 1930s. When she was older and reflecting back on her life, she said, "The people used routes that they had used for many years. The Dene didn't know about this place [her community in Saskatchewan at

Looking north up Nueltin Lake.

the time, in 1978] or the south. They only lived up north. They only traveled in the North. People didn't need to travel south because they relied on caribou, and the caribou were in the North. People lived on caribou so they lived on the edge of the barrenlands." In this manner, the Dene had occupied the vast arc of land from Churchill northwest to nearby the mouth of the Coppermine River, the sweeping forest-tundra transition zone, for millennia.* Nueltin, in fact, was close to the eastern edge of their traditional territory.

▿   ▿   ▿   ▿   ▿

* Anthropologist June Helm has described "the topographic grasp of the Great Slave drainage and the transfers to the major drainages into marine [sea] waters" as being at the heart of Dene knowledge, by which she refers to their mental mapping of the Great Slave Lake area, the rivers flowing in and out of it, and the overland routes to other rivers that in turn flow down to the sea (e.g., Coppermine, Burnside, Back, and Thelon), some of which they had followed to the mouth. Early maps drawn by Dene show Great Slave Lake as the focal point, with numerous rivers running to the sea toward both the north and the east.

To Inuit, it is Qikiqtariaktuk, the Lake with Many Islands. Nueltin is effectively a place of overlap for Dene and Inuit. All of the lakes and rivers and landmarks in the surrounding country, known so well by Dene, also have Inuktitut names. This is not uncommon, but it is probably more pronounced in this small region of northern Manitoba and southern Nunavut than anywhere else in Canada. The history of this overlap is anything but uneventful. One thing is clear—it has a lot do with the caribou.

In the late 1600s and early 1700s, there was a general drift southward of Inuit both along the west coast of Hudson Bay and possibly overland from the Arctic coast inland toward the Thelon River. The motives behind this were the usual for a nomadic hunting people: the incessant search for food resources and better living conditions. It was a cooling period,* climatically speaking, so the Inuit methodologies for survival continued to prove applicable as they moved south, and food in particular (wood also, for the people venturing inland) was notably easier to obtain. Moving south would eventually, of course, bring them in contact with the Caribou-Eater Chipewyans, of whom they probably had little or no previous experience at this point, whose habits and way of life were very different in many ways (though caribou became central to both), and with whom they could not speak—all of which is a recipe for tension, if not hostility. These ancestors of today's Dene had been living and hunting in the tundra-forest transition region for nearly 2,500 years and venturing well out onto the barrenlands in pursuit of the caribou.

By coincidence, in 1717 the Hudson's Bay Company established a trading post at what is now Churchill. Just two years before that, the HBC had sent an emissary, William Stuart, accompanied by a young Chipewyan woman, Thanadelthur, and several Cree men, on a mission to establish peace between the more southerly Cree and the more northerly Chipewyan. Both groups had suffered from mutually hostile sentiments. This peace effort was successful so

* This period is often referred to as the Little Ice Age.

that henceforth both groups were able to trade with the HBC, which led in part to the establishment of the post at Churchill. It also planted the idea of exploring far to the northwest, where Thanadelthur told the HBC men they would find large deposits of copper; fifty years later, Samuel Hearne set off on exactly this quest.

If there were fear, uncertainty, and anxiety expressed as hostility between Cree and Chipewyan, then one can imagine that similar feelings were inevitable when Inuit came into contact with either group. That is almost certainly what happened next. At this time, Inuit were living along the coast of Hudson Bay, as far south as the present community of Arviat, but were not making extensive use of the adjacent inland territory. Inuit contact with the Dene, who stayed inland for the most part, was therefore very limited until the Inuit were drawn into trade at the new post in Churchill. This signalled the dawn of a new era. In the post journal, written at Churchill on April 16, 1721, the factor described his efforts to foster a friendly relationship between Dene and Inuit.

> I have been a Discoursing yᵉ Northoran Indians againe. For to be brisk in Hunting & gotting of furrs by going into ye Woods up in ye Countrey & not to Keep by ye Sea Side and in yᵉ barren plaines; and if they see any Esquimoues thay should not Meddle wᵗʰ them thay being our friends, thay Reply'd yt Last Summer... had made a peace wᵗʰ them; thay saying yt thay Traded together thay giving them Knives and alls, ye other Returning small Copper Lances & arrow heads.

By this account, according to the Chipewyan, who also reported, somewhat dubiously, a bloody encounter just the year before, the two groups had engaged in friendly trade, though it is not known where this occurred or even if it refers specifically to the Inuit living along the Hudson Bay coast. The factor, however, wanted peace and suggested the Dene avoid hunting and taking furs in what could be construed as Inuit territory.

A few years later, in June of 1725, a large group of one hundred Dene came to Churchill and complained to the factor about Inuit aggression that, allegedly, had occurred much farther to the north up the Hudson Bay coast. "Ye Esquemoys had been to war with them & had Murdered Severall of them...then they askt me whether they must Stand Still & be Knockt on the head Like Doggs or fight in their own Defence or now by Reason we had ordered them not to war with any Natives." There is no explanation as to why the Dene were so far north, right by the sea, nor any real indication of how familiar they were with the coast itself, quite far removed from their usual hunting grounds farther inland.

In an attempt to quell these ongoing hostilities, such as they were, the HBC began to send a sloop along the Hudson Bay coast for the specific purpose of trade with the Inuit. This, they hoped, would lead to less confrontation between the two groups coming to trade at Churchill (by then the more substantial Fort Prince of Wales), though they also sent two Chipewyan men along on the ship with the stated desire that they "Endeavor to contact a Friendship Between their Country Man and the Eskemaux." The Chipewyan resented this arrangement, perceiving that Inuit were receiving preferential treatment, having the trade brought to them, so to speak, whereas the Dene were forced to walk overland for many miles to the "stone house" at Fort Prince of Wales. Why, they argued, could they not also trade with the ship when it stopped at Eskimo Point and nearby Knapp Bay, for those locations would be much more convenient for them as well.

In 1755, a Chipewyan trading party left Fort Prince of Wales headed north along the coast. Why they chose this route is uncertain.* When the HBC sloop passed by offshore, they signalled it with smoke, hoping to trade the large stock of caribou meat accumulated by their recent hunts, but the Englishmen ignored them—arguably for good reason, not knowing the inshore waters there and not having on board the usual trade goods associated

---

* Some, including Samuel Hearne, believed the Chipewyan went north seeking revenge. Two Chipewyan leaders had perished the previous winter, and some records suggest that Dene at the time believed Inuit brought misfortune upon their enemies by magic, thereby causing sickness and death and even keeping the caribou away from Dene hunters.

with the Chipewyan—and sailed on by to trade with Inuit at Eskimo Point. This infuriated the Chipewyan, as they lay in wait, watching first the Inuit engage in trading transactions and then the sloop weigh anchor to sail away northward. At that moment, they set upon the Inuit camp of four tents and murdered everyone, man, woman, and child, at least sixteen in all. The sloop's captain stopped in on his return voyage and discovered a ghastly scene: "aparall lying both of the men and the womens all tore. . . . Several of their bones lying about their tent poles and tents lying all in a heap." Not one survived.

After this attack, the Inuit abandoned the site and did not return to the Eskimo Point area for several years. When they did return in 1764, they established a truce with the Dene, and the following year the HBC sloop was back, this time trading with both Inuit and Dene at Eskimo Point. More than a hundred people in all, roughly two-thirds Dene and one-third Inuit, were present at the event. So convivial was the contact that two years later two Inuit families spent the winter with their new Dene friends in the sparsely wooded country halfway between Eskimo Point and Churchill. The peaceful trading arrangement at Eskimo Point continued more or less annually for the next several years,* Inuit and Dene becoming ever more comfortable with each other, until Fort Prince of Wales was captured by the French in 1782.

That same year, during the winter of 1781 to 1782, a smallpox epidemic swept through the Chipewyan population, killing nearly half. Around this time, new trading posts were being established inland, mostly by the North West Company, near Lake Athabasca, just to the west of the Caribou-Eater Chipewyan territory, providing an alternative for their trade. For all of these reasons, the move-

---

* In the middle of this period, during the summer of 1771, the most famous massacre of all occurred at Bloody Falls on the Coppermine River, witnessed by Samuel Hearne and involving at least some of these same Churchill-based Chipewyan. Evidently, there remained tensions between Dene and Inuit in some quarters.

ment pattern of the Chipewyan shifted away from the Hudson Bay coast, and therefore contact with Inuit decreased. After Samuel Hearne reestablished the HBC presence at Churchill, following the Treaty of Paris (1783), the HBC sloop renewed its trading voyages along the Hudson Bay coast in 1785. Both Inuit and Chipewyan again used the opportunity to trade at Eskimo Point, and the relationships between them remained peaceful. Those voyages continued until 1790. After that, Inuit wishing to trade needed to travel down to Churchill where, of course, contact with Chipewyan was virtually certain. An HBC census from 1838 documents that the Churchill post was frequented by 663 Inuit, 429 Chipewyan, and 34 Cree. A post that was originally established to serve the Chipewyan had become equally if not more important to the Inuit for trade.

The traders encouraged Inuit to continue bringing furs and caribou meat and began to request whales as well. In return, the Inuit began to acquire rifles and fishnets, two major assets in their quest for survival on the land. As the century turned, this new technology allowed the Inuit to range farther afield and survive more easily. The acquisition of these trade goods permitted the Inuit to shift inland on a more permanent basis, drawn by the security of the vast herds of caribou. In making this move, they began to penetrate the traditional territory of the Caribou-Eater Chipewyan, the region surrounding Nueltin Lake, and north and northwest from there. It was probably the 1830s or 1840s before significant numbers of Inuit moved far enough inland to effectively cut off their own easy access to the sea on a long-term basis. By the same time, numbers of the Chipewyan had been dramatically decreased by disease, and those remaining had withdrawn somewhat to the south. In a sense, the land was available for the taking by Inuit. One must remember, however, that neither of these cultures held the concept of land ownership. In any case, there is no indication that the Chipewyan resisted this change. Rather, the two groups began to come together for annual gatherings on both the Kazan and Thelon rivers, gatherings that were opportunities for trade. As Aningaat, an old Inuit man in Arviat, who is now deceased, said some years ago, "Eskimos and Indians long ago have found a way to live in peace in our country; the adoption of a child was the token of lasting friendship."

As a result of this ongoing contact, Fr. Gasté, in the summer 1868, was aware that if he followed the old way north from Reindeer Lake to the barrenlands with the Caribou-Eater Chipewyan, he would encounter Inuit. He was the first missionary to do so. Clearly, by that time the Inuit were well established along the Kazan River. When some of these Inuit accompanied Fr. Gasté back to Lac du Brochet on the same route, they discovered a trading post that was, in fact, more easily accessible than the Churchill post they had been using until then. Over the next three decades, their travel to the Dene community at Lac du Brochet and their interactions with the Dene living and hunting along the well-worn travel route continued to increase. The HBC census in 1881 indicates that there were 217 Inuit who belonged to the Brochet post, along with 386 Chipewyan. The corresponding numbers for Churchill that same year were 515 Inuit and 157 Chipewyan, both less than in 1838, a mark of the transition that had occurred. In 1894, when Tyrrell descended the Kazan River, he estimated the Inuit population along that river at approximately one thousand. Over the three or four decades following 1880, the Caribou Inuit flourished. They extended south right to the treeline. The Dene, by contrast, had contracted their territory, venturing out onto the barrenlands with a much lower frequency.

It seems fair to say that the vast inland area between the Kazan River and Hudson Bay, north as far as Yathkyed Lake (notably a Dene name), had previously been largely Chipewyan territory— when Hearne, during his barrenlands trek in 1770, crossed Nueltin Lake and then the Kazan River, he encountered no Inuit but many Chipewyans. Their full range extended all the way northwest to the Thelon valley and beyond. During the following decades, that changed. The transition continued into the nineteenth century, and by 1850, one could reasonably say that much of the same territory was now predominantly occupied by Inuit. The relationship between the two peoples has remained peaceable ever since, though it took some time for the fears and uncertainties to subside. When Tyrrell was preparing to set off down the Dubawnt River in 1893 (just one year before his Kazan trip), the Chipewyan whom he attempted to engage declined, saying, "We would meet with great impassable canyons, and that the country through which [the river] flowed was inhabited by savage tribes of Eskimos, who would undoubtedly eat us."

The interactions between Inuit and Dene continued, most particularly in the area immediately surrounding Nueltin Lake. As this place became a focal point for the fox trapping boom of the 1920s and 1930s, Inuit and Dene often met at the numerous trading posts that popped up all over the Country. On many occasions, they helped each other out. Old Dene trappers recalled those days with a smile. Alex Montgrand, born in 1901, now deceased, remembered a trip by dog team in the 1920s north to the area of Kasba and Ennadai lakes on the Kazan River. He recalled staying with Inuit for a few days, enjoying their hospitality, dancing, and games. "They were dancing, beating drums, so we danced with them." His traveling partner on that trip, Ross Cummings, born in 1889, claimed to know some Inuktitut, reflecting, "They were good people who really knew how to survive."

In the period from 1915 to 1925, the barrenlands caribou herds were decimated by changeable winter weather when the lichens they depended on for food became repeatedly encrusted in ice. The surviving caribou went elsewhere, and two-thirds of the Inuit who depended upon them died of starvation.

Those who survived did well in the late 1920s and 1930s. Trapping for white fox during those boom years became a mainstay of their survival, and the caribou returned. They were relatively good years. A Dene man, Leon Medal, born in 1913, who passed away in 1989, remembered meeting Inuit during a trapping season on the barrenlands.

At Ennadai Lake you know, 1929, there were lots of Eskimos
there. Oh about close to a hundred families there. That time
I saw a snowhouse. An Eskimo house is called *yath koé* in
Chipewyan.

The Eskimo would make a fire. There was no big wood, and
no gas stove at that time. He had a big kettle and would make
tea, that's all. He doesn't cook the meat. He just eats it that
way. I never tried it myself.

At that time I was a young boy, 18 years old. I started talking English but the Eskimo didn't understand. So we just
talked Chipewyan that time. I stayed with him for two days.
He gave me some tobacco and some candles, everything. This
was at Ennadai Lake, just across from the sandbar. That's the
place where there still lots of Eskimos. They hunted lots of
caribou in small canoes. This Eskimo he killed lots and gave
me lots for dog food.

But the Eskimo, he used a lot of dogs. For one dogteam he
runs sometimes twenty dogs. He fed those dogs caribou. There
was lots of caribou. And the fishing was good too. The Eskimo
is a good hunter that one. They're smart guys too you know.

About the same time, 1929, Jimmy Dzeylion, son of Lac du
Brochet's famous Alphonse Dzeylion, traveled north with his father
and other Dene, and they too met Inuit.

There would be a big feast. The Dene would provide a bull
caribou for the feast. This caribou had been killed in the fall so
it was partly rotted. The Dene would make tea using a very
large pail, maybe 20 gallons, for the feast. The fire was just a
small fire with one slow burning big log. Then all the men
would come to the feast. Women were not invited. The fat bull
caribou was taken to where the feast was. The Eskimo would
cut thin strips with a big knife, or they would use an axe. This
caribou was not cooked, but frozen. After twenty minutes of
eating the tea was passed around, sometimes by a few women,
with cups handed to everyone. There were about twenty men
at the feast I remember. After the men ate, then some of the
women would eat too. I didn't like to see our women eating
raw meat. The Eskimo eat like dogs to us but this is their way
of life and it's okay by me.

Jean Baptiste Merasty, still living in Brochet, also remembers meeting Inuit at Nueltin Lake a few years later in 1945. About twenty-five families of very hungry Inuit, as he recalled, were relocated by airplane from farther north, near the Kazan River, to an island in Nueltin Lake. "I don't know why they put them on an island," he said. "They only had one little canoe for fishing. They were very poor. Lots of children too. They stayed all that summer. They asked the Dene there [including Merasty] to help move them to the mainland, which we did." In the fall the Dene went south down to Brochet, and when they returned the next summer, the Inuit had gone. "Those Inuit would have starved if the Dene had not helped them. I stayed with them overnight. They were just like any other humans." So far as Merasty knows, the Inuit left Nueltin and walked back to their own camps by the Kazans (which in fact is correct).

Nueltin Lake, meeting place of Dene and Inuit, before and after the white man's arrival, remained a place with a particular spirit, alive in both cultures. When the white man came—both canoeists and trappers—that did not change. In fact, still today, when neither Dene nor Inuit, neither trapper nor canoeist, spends more than a few days in a year on the shores of Nueltin, it remains the symbolic meeting place of the two original cultures of the barrenlands, the two peoples whose very lives depended on the caribou. It is the caribou, above all, that define this landscape, as they continue their life-giving migrations, north in the spring and south in the fall, to and fro past the shores of Nueltin Lake. The spirit of Mother Nonucho, evidently, lives on.

◁ ▷   ◁ ▷   ◁ ▷   ◁ ▷   ◁ ▷   ◁ ▷   ◁ ▷   ◁ ▷   ◁ ▷

A Modern Paddler's Perspective

Nueltin to the Bay

Paddling Nueltin Lake from south to north, you make a transition from one world to the next. A paddler today watches as the forests alongside thin. Less hardy tree species—white spruce, paper birch, and jack pine—quickly thin out and soon vanish. The odd tamarack still bravely stands in low sheltered creeks, the bark and branches on their north side stripped away by the ferocious northern winter winds. Tundra birch are less a tree than a low ground-hugging shrub. Black spruce predominate, but it is clear that they are struggling to survive and are on the extreme edge of their range. They take on odd gnarled shapes looking strangely deformed. Huddled in tight-knit clumps seeking protection from cold winds, they form dense-knit copses so tight a small bird can easily remain warm and dry even in the fiercest storms. These short trees belie their age. If you look closely, you will see that at ground level a six-foot tree can easily have a twenty-inch girth. Hills are covered with wild jumbles of boulder—from basketball to television to automobile sized—covered with gray and black and green lichens. Other boulders wear splashes of bright yellow, orange, and red lichens that might fool a passer-by into thinking someone had painted them. Permafrost lies just under the surface, and the lower areas are all wet morasses of hummocky grasses and peat. The white-silver blooms of cotton grass that cover endless acres can easily fool one's eye into believing that they are looking at a gentle windswept pond.

Along the route you pass a long flat-topped sandy island now called Indian Camp Island. This is the Sleeping Island from which the lake derived its name. Walking its length today, paddlers find the remains of many Dene camps.

The trout in tundra lakes are such as you have never seen before. The waters cool as you head north. No need here for lake trout to seek out deeper cold water as they do in southern reaches. Here they stay "up top" all year. To fish here will ruin you for life. It's less fishing than hunting as you wait and watch for a dorsal fin to break the surface where the trout graze on dead insects. As you paddle along, you see mile after mile of thick rafts of mosquitoes and midges and blackflies on the water's surface. A quick cast almost always guarantees a fish for lunch or at least a look at a huge monster following your hook to the side of your canoe. The meat—for it is meat—is so firm you have to cut it with a knife even after it is cooked. And the steady diet of insects gives the fillets a bright red color and a faint sweet taste.

Nueltin Lake drops into Sealhole Lake by two separate main channels. It is obvious from Oberholtzer's journal that they found the southernmost channel. The northern channel is an easy S-turn in class II water while the southern channel is a less easy route. Here you are presented with a midstream island that constricts the extremely fast current into two channels. The south channel is the longer of the two and is a shallow curve with randomly scattered boulders ready to pounce and eat a canoe. The north channel is narrower and soon leads to a small torrential ledge that cannot be paddled. Paddlers today are wise to portage past this ledge across the island and to continue the carry farther on.

Not far on downstream is a wild rapid easily classed a III by paddlers today. It is an S-turn that requires two full front ferries from side to side through fast current and big waves. Alternately you can paddle like mad in midriver and hope you don't swamp in two- and three-foot white-capped waves.

Halfway through Nueltin Lake, heading north,
you leave the trees behind upon entering the barrenlands,
and the hillsides are covered with a jumble of boulders.

From Sealhole to Hudson Bay is nearly two hundred miles. Over that distance the river drops nine hundred feet, implying a steady run of current. Initially, here, the Thlewiaza River allows today's paddler to practice their skill on the barrens. Heading nearly straight east, it seems to wind its way in and out of a sparse treeline that offers the relative comfort of fire and shelter if it is needed. Gone now are the gentle sand beaches with table-top camping behind. Here, the river runs in a gentle valley between inviting-looking banks covered in soft green. But walking into this green beauty quickly dispels any idea of camping. It is always boggy sedge that makes camping all but impossible. Unless you are lucky enough to find a rare dry, low spot near shore, you are forced to hike to the top of the riverbanks far up from the water. In some sections the river cuts its way through rocky, sandy hills, leaving near vertical scrambles to the top. Often at the top, a camper will find nothing but a maze of boulders packed so close together that camping is virtually impossible. This is an inhospitable landscape.

But there is much beauty on this stretch of the Thlewiaza. Many gorgeous eskers and gentle fast rapids speed you along as you float under a sunny sky. After Edehon Lake the river picks up speed. The force of spring breakup is evident, and one can see why the Inuit call this Kuujuaq, or Big River. Often at the top of the riverbanks, thirty or forty feet above, you can see where ice has scoured away willows and piled up mounds of dirt and rock. Midriver piles of scraped-up rock appear each spring and then vanish the next spring. Larger islands have their upstream edges covered with giant walls of boulders. The islands tend to be higher on the upstream edge and taper lower toward the end where the river deposits sand and silt scoured from the leading edge of the island. The islands are literally migrating downstream year after year. The river here tends to be in a deep channel with steep, high loose-gravel banks and is often a series of giant sweeping S-turns. The outsides of the turns are deep, with a fast current next to the shore. On each outside turn, long boulder fans point downstream, left where the ice deposited them, in formations that look like the work of heavy machinery. Behind these giant fans are calm eddy pools, and here you can often catch a river trout or a grayling. The current in the lower river easily runs to speeds of seven miles per hour, speeding you with great haste toward the mouth at Hudson Bay.

Run to the Sea

Nueltin is a big lake. Oberholtzer and Magee had not enjoyed good weather during their transit of its one-hundred-mile length. They had repeatedly found themselves paddling up long dead-end bays. It took them two weeks to overcome the challenges of Nueltin. On August 28, they found themselves making a three-hundred-yard portage around one of several rapids where the Thlewiaza exits from Nueltin. Every canoeist knows the dichotomous feeling that comes with reentering the river after a long lake crossing. On the one hand, there is relief to feel the current tugging again at the canoe. On the other hand, there is the nagging uncertainty about the rapids, derived from the absence of fast-water practice for several days. Within the first mile of this, the final stretch of the Thlewiaza, as Oberholtzer recorded, they had a serious problem.

▷ ▷ *Here we had our first real mishap. I misjudged the distance between the shore and a certain protruding rock, round which the water has a big fall. It looked wide enough, but when we tried it for the second time, the canoe stuck tight and quickly filled with water. I was already bare to my knees but Billy could not let go the rope and so I had to jump in just as I was. The water flooded, in over the packs, even while I was hurling them ashore; and the good things that were being lost in each one flashed across my mind—all my pictures, my camera, the notebooks, the cask of tea, the hardtack in the jumbo pack, and finally (when all else was ashore) the beans. I was sure they had gone, but no, there they were on shore; and I must have taken them out. Then I saw the bag of pots and plates lodged in the stern and ready to ride away. I thought of our food without pans and once more I jumped in just in time to save*

147

the cooking utensils. We could not pull the canoe back. It was full of water and wedged tight. When we pried it loose it turned over and Billy came tumbling over the rocks to hold the rope. Then we bailed the canoe out and took stock of our damages.

They were cold and wet, as was some of their food, and they had lost the rifle. Even though they had not been using it much—it is difficult to understand why they were not eating caribou regularly—as the trip progressed and their food supplied dwindled, the rifle would have been a valued piece of insurance. Now it was gone.

The next couple of days were sheer misery. "I hardly knew what to do. There was not a sheltered place nor a stick of wood in sight; the lake was running high and we were both cold." On top of which, they were unable to travel beyond a small lake just downstream

The rapid in the Thlewiaza where Oberholtzer and Magee had their "first real mishap," which looks much the same today as it did in 1912.

from their mishap. They tried to sleep under the overturned canoe but spent much of their time cold and wet.

▷ ▷ *Friday, August 30. After a high south-east wind all night, the real rain set in at daylight. It dripped a little from the side of the canoe but did no harm. I was very tired of my narrow bed and poor covers. All I could see on the lake was white caps and the gray mist blotting out the shores and making the lake appear very large.... The wind was driving the cold mist before it in a gale. When we ran down the beach to find a sheltered spot for a fire, Billy, shrivelled and shivering, crouched beneath some spruce bushes hardly able to hold his matches, while I chopped pieces out of the old wigwam poles. At last we got it going and heaped on all the roots and twisted branches we could find. Then we had a good breakfast of oatmeal and pemmican hash. The day was desolate and chilling. Still in the fine driving rain, we put up the sail as a partial shelter; and presently Billy went back to bed while I hugged the fire for a little warmth, drying one side while the other got wet.*

▷ ▷ *Saturday August 31. I was very uncomfortable all night. Some time in my half-sleep I drew out my legs and stretched them out in the rain. My knees ached badly and I was cold, the mist came in the side a little.... When I got up at six the breakers were racing in against the stony shore and the sky was still leaden with mist. We made our fire on the other side of the sail and with less trouble than on the morning before, but the wind blew through most annoyingly. My eyes were red with smoke, my eyelashes singed, my nose and hands scratched, and my trousers full of holes. Besides, though it was not raining much, the ground was covered with little pools of water and every bush was dripping.*

The next morning, September 1, by which date Oberholtzer had hoped to be at Churchill, the weather permitted their departure from this miserable scene. By six o'clock in the morning, the canoe was underway. In no time at all, they found themselves being pulled along again by the swift current of the Thlewiaza. Though they continued steadily downstream, progress was slowed regularly by portages and shallow rapids where they were forced to wade. On September 5, Oberholtzer offered a rare hint of his growing concern.

▷ ▷ *I read again Mr. Tyrrell's report and realized how serious our position was beginning to look. Bad weather was undoubtedly near and we had no notion how far we were from Churchill. Probably the worst of the Barren Lands was to come and we were travelling hardly more than five miles a day and both of us rheumatic.*

The next day he added an even more somber note.

▷ ▷ *The prospects for reaching home or even Churchill before winter look very dark, but I am resolved to make a desperate try.*

For two days the weather pinned them down. The future seemed even more dismal. On September 7, they awoke again to rain and fog.

▷ ▷ *Very dreary in the tent; clothes damp, ground soggy, feet cold, rain pattering on top of tent and dripping down the sides like a leaking pipe, light dreary.*

That afternoon the rain stopped and the mist retreated, and at three o'clock they set off once again, ever uncertain of how much farther they had to paddle before reaching Hudson Bay or what challenges awaited them there. Now they picked up speed; the current pushed them along; even a tailwind rose to help out. They saw caribou on the shore and seals in the water and birds everywhere. Oberholtzer's sense heightened that the sea must be near. But how near? That evening the sky cleared, and he observed the shimmering aurora borealis. Long days of paddling and portaging and uncertainty continued, but at least they were moving downstream, secure in the knowledge that eventually the river must lead to the sea. In fact, they were lucky with the weather. It did not snow, as it easily can at this time of year. It was not even very cold. On one occasion, Oberholtzer commented how warm it was, writing, "A beautiful clear hot day, the warmest perhaps since we left the Saskatchewan [River]."

To describe their final descent of the Thlewiaza would be to offer a repetitive litany of discomfort and anxiety, of rapids and portages, of wind and rain, of blackflies and mosquitoes, and of failing confidence. Stopped for supper on an island, Oberholtzer wrote, "In hunting for wood I found an old drifted toboggan runner.* We had seen three cranes. On the beach I found two shells—one of them pink and fluted, which Billy said could never go farther than three miles from the sea." Their newfound optimism was rewarded at last, and rewarded in a way they had no reason—or even right—to expect.

▷ ▷ *Friday, September 12. The river quickly broadened to a mile or more and we soon saw with fresh hope a great opening before us. Low, stoney shores and islands—with grasses all yellow and brown. Soon after I had tasted the water, Billy saw two queer curling columns shifting against the gray eastern sky. If not smoke, he said, he had never seen anything like them before. Then, while we were marveling at the phenomenon, I saw something black moving on the water and presently there was a boat coming toward us. I saw at once that it was an eskimo in his kayak. Swinging his double paddle slowly from side to side and with two little red flannel streamers from each end of his boat, he came up beside us, and extending his paddle for me to take hold of, shook hands.*

As simply as that, Oberholtzer described what was without doubt the luckiest event of their entire journey. The two paddlers,

---

* This runner must have been from an Inuit sled, or *qamutik* (also *kamotik*), that had they known, would have been another sign that the coast was nearby.

after seventy-nine days of often arduous travel, arriving on the bleak and dangerous shore of Hudson Bay in mid-September, were fortunate enough to encounter an Inuit family at the mouth of the Thlewiaza. To the Inuit this place was (and still is) Aglirnaqtuq. It was a place of plenty, where seals and whales and fish—and a short walk inland, caribou—would give you everything you needed to survive in comfort. But to two weary and unfamiliar travelers from the south, this place was the most desolate and inhospitable on Earth. The Inuk in his *qajaq* introduced himself. Oberholtzer recorded his name, first as "Pike" and later, more correctly, as "Bite." Bite was exceedingly hospitable, helping to unload their canoe, arranging some shelter for them, offering food and warmth. Oberholtzer and Magee were invited into Bite's tent, where his wife was tending to the baby and the family's needs. Within hours he changed his own family's plan—they were headed north—and agreed to sail south in order to deliver Oberholtzer and Magee to Churchill, a trip of four days, he predicted. Oberholtzer immedi-

In Oberholtzer's own words, on September 12 at the mouth of the Thlewiaza: "I saw at once that it was an eskimo in his kayak. Swinging his double paddle slowly from side to side and with two little red flannel streamers from each end of his boat, he came up beside us, and extending his paddle for me to take hold of, shook hands."

ately offered gifts of tobacco, a pipe, a knife, and some tea and sugar. The arrangement was thus cemented, with very few words. The coincidence that delivered Bite to this place at this time, as he traveled by boat north up the coast from Churchill, was nothing short of providential. Had either party's travel schedules varied by just one day, they could easily have missed each other. Oberholtzer's only apparent concession to this good fortune was to write in his journal, "All our troubles now seemed over and I thought ourselves truly blessed." Indeed. Had they not met someone at Aglirnaqtuq, their survival would have been in doubt, at the very least.

As it was, the journey by boat was not straightforward, certainly not easy, but compared to what Oberholtzer and Magee would have faced alone in their canoe, it was a Sunday stroll in the park. When bad weather detained the voyage, the family simply made camp, made everyone comfortable, and entertained themselves. Oberholtzer clearly relished the opportunity to observe.

▷ ▷ *All of them were smiling in spite of adversity and the baby throve on kisses and rough caresses—the rougher the better. Pike's wife baked three bannocks on the bare stove top while the big boy tended the bare bottomed baby. The more violently he rocked it, the more it laughed. It had on its head a hood festooned with black and white beads. The second boy carried the telescope in a red flannel bag decorated with a snake of black and white beads. Mother playing with her youngest boy. She would show her teeth and pretend to cry and when he pulled open her eyes and found them smiling, both would laugh. He had pulled his shirt over his head and wore only a blue helmeted hat. He had a great round protruding belly and navel and was light brown all over except his pink face and feet and hands and the places he had scratched gray.*

As they traveled, Oberholtzer made occasional notes on the members of the family. Bite's wife: "Tah-he-oh chanted to her baby. Variable expressive face. Happy disposition." The oldest boy: "Oo-too-pul-yak dwarfish in features and limbs. Short, stubby fingers. Long soft black hair covering the forehead and ears and framing his face with curves. Dirtiest and most ragged big brother and big sister of the family. Very affectionate to little ones." The younger boy, who took to sucking on the gifted pipe: "Oh-rut-yuk resembles his mother. Oval face with even-colored deep pink cheeks. Hair cut rather short to the temples and thin features regular. Mischievous way of looking out of the corners of his eyes and shrewdly smiling."

Partway to Churchill, Bite pulled in to another Inuit camp where, as Oberholtzer discerned, he planned to leave his family while he completed the mission to Churchill. In camp overnight they feasted on duck and Arctic char, and Oberholtzer's newly relaxed state of mind led to his waxing poetically on the beauty of the evening.

▷ ▷ *Sunday, September 15. The wind had almost died and the afternoon was beautifully warm. Light clouds of many colors were filling the sky and the earlier turquoise of the bay had turned to a purple gray. The sunset shone golden on the rippling waters near shore.*

Ahmak's camp, with caribou-skin tent,
where Bite and party stopped en route to Churchill.

The headman in this camp was Ahmak, "erect, stalwart, straight, broad-shouldered, active, agile," and his helpful son Kin-mick-kee, "a bonny boy," as Oberholtzer recorded. Delayed again by weather, they fairly luxuriated in this camp. No one was pressed; nobody expressed any concern about the passage of time or the evident delay for Bite and his family on their intended trip to the north. All was well with the world.

▷ ▷ *Monday, September 16th. . . . The boys lent a hand and everybody was very merry. The morning was dry and, in spite of the wind, not cold. In the afternoon the children were all out playing—the biggest and the youngest together. They went over to the nearest one and sailed their little wooden boats. The sails were made of shavings and one of the boats had been hollowed out of a large piece of wood with much labor. Oo-too-put-yak, in spite of the chilly wind, waded in barefoot. This is a laborious life. I saw the old woman go over for a big load of sticks, which she carried on her back, hobbling along with two sticks.*

The voyage to Churchill, as it eventually unfolded, was a happy and memorable experience for Oberholtzer. They tried towing the canoe behind Bite's boat but eventually had to pull it on board and tie it down. The Inuit cooked some whale meat, which did not appeal to the uninitiated—and probably helped to induce a feeling of seasickness during the rolling swells—but as the journal indicates, "Every time the canoe had to be changed or the sail altered, there was great merriment and the good humor was infectious."

On September 19, a full week after the two travelers had arrived at the mouth of the Thlewiaza, the boat sailed into the mouth of the Churchill River. "At last, just at dusk, we sighted land and, half an hour later, in the wildest confusion, we dropped anchor [in] Button Bay among the breakers at the west side of a bay." In no time, it seems, they were ashore.

▷ ▷ *. . . a short walk from the fort. Accordingly, we all started across the rocks and bogs and creeks with our personal packs. Finally, we*

came to a path which led over to a number of lighted buildings.
I was guided to one of them and, at knocking, found myself face to
face with a lady, who said the H.B.C., was miles away. Her hus-
band, Major Demers* of the Mounted Police, sent us over to the
barracks where Constable Rose got out of bed, made supper, and
gave us a royal welcome.

In his monthly report to the commissioner of the Royal North
West Mounted Police, Superintendent Demers stated that "on
September 17th *[sic]*, Mr. E. C. Oberholtzer, a journalist from
Davenport, Iowa, U.S.A., arrived at Churchill; he came via Le Pas,
Reindeer Lake, Cochrane River and the Thlewiaza River, to Hud-
son Bay. He had only one Indian with him, and travelled the whole
distance in a canoe."

⏤ ⏤ ⏤ ⏤ ⏤

Christian Leden, a self-centered Norwegian, sailed into Churchill
on the HBC ship the *Nascopie* in the summer of 1913, just a year
after Oberholtzer, in search of romantic adventure among "the
Eskimos." In his account of the experience, originally published
in German, he nonetheless offered a timely description of the
outpost.

"Near the sea, the grey-white walls of Fort Prince of Wales are
gleaming in the sun—overgrown with moss and romantic—a
reminder of vanished times telling of the urge to discover, of the
spirit of adventure and of the lust for conquest over the northern
race. A few old cannon stand there on the walls and ramparts
overgrown with heather and willow."

One has to believe he was applying much of his own sentiment
and motivation to the early days of the Hudson's Bay Company,
whose men established the old fort as a trading post in 1717. It was
from here that Samuel Hearne began his remarkable trek across
the barrenlands, to the mouth of the Coppermine River, from

---

* Actually, they met Superintendent François Demers of the Royal North
West Mounted Police.

1769 to 1772. It was from here that ships had sailed north along the coast of Hudson Bay, in attempts to bring the coastal Inuit into the fur trade.

At the time of Oberholtzer's and Leden's visits, the local population of non-Native people consisted of the Hudson's Bay Company employees, the Royal North West Mounted Police, the Anglican missionary, and their respective families. Life was not that much different for these people from what it had been for their predecessors of the previous century. The police station was located nearby the river mouth. The HBC post and the missionary's house were situated about two and a half miles upstream.

᭝ ᭝ ᭝ ᭝ ᭝

The morning after their arrival, everyone made their way over to the Hudson's Bay Company post, where Oberholtzer hoped to meet the factor and make some arrangements.

▷ ▷ *I went in through the gate and knocked at the front door, over which a fine pair of antlers was hanging. Mr. Sevier,* the clergyman, let me in and he and his wife gave me a fine tea and entertained me for an hour till the company sent down to say that the eskimos had arrived. I went up at once with Mr. Sevier and met Mr. Handford of the company. He explained that eskimo wages were very low and said he did not believe in spoiling the men. From his house we went over with the eskimos to the store. Thirty skins were doled out to Bite but he was not satisfied and had to be given forty. To Ah-mat I gave ten skins and to each some presents of candy and tobacco and ample provisions for the return trip.*

That night the first frost of the season fell upon Churchill. The weather turned foul. Discussion focused now on the journey ahead. The two men realized it was in their best interest to keep moving south, as they held onto hope of returning home before winter.

---

* The Reverend F. C. Severier was an Anglican minister.

Oberholtzer bought supplies and new clothing for both himself and Magee. All in, for these personal needs, plus the payments to Bite and Ahmak and a few gifts for his various hosts, the bill at the HBC was ninety-five dollars.* He could not have begun to pay Bite true value for his services—in all likelihood, Oberholtzer owed his life to this Inuk.

---

* In 1912, Cdn$95 would have been equivalent to Cdn$1,780 in 2007.

Arviat

It feels like early winter, on September 26, 2006, when the small twin-engine plane takes off from Rankin Inlet, halfway up the west coast of Hudson Bay, for the short hop south to Arviat. As the plane swooped down the coast of Hudson Bay, I could see thick fog rolling inland from the sea, generated by the cold water of Hudson Bay contacting the even colder air of the wintry winds above. There was some question as to whether conditions would permit us to land, but as so often happens up north, a superior pilot found his way down, despite the decidedly iffy conditions, through the odd combination of wind and fog, to put us safely on the ground.

No matter how you tackle it, it's a long way to Arviat. I chose to fly north to Iqaluit, west to Rankin Inlet, and then south to Arviat. I could have gone around the other way, so to speak, flying first to Winnipeg, then north to Churchill, and on to Arviat. Each route has its advantages and disadvantages, and each works better on different days of the week. Travel in the far north is like a board game from my youth, Snakes and Ladders, with a never-ending series of ups and downs, setbacks and leaps forward. This time, when I switched planes in Iqaluit (after a four-hour layover) for my flight to Rankin Inlet (where I had an overnight layover), my luggage was switched onto a different plane going farther north to a small village on the Melville Peninsula, well north of the Arctic Circle. It would be at least seventy-two hours before there was any chance of seeing that bag again, I was told by the airline, and in fact it took so long that I was without it for my entire time in Arviat—the bag arrived on the same plane I was to board for the flight home, a week later. That, as I have come to expect during thirty years of Arctic travel, is just part of life in the North. Fortunately, I had been prudent enough to put all the project-related material, which I *really* needed during the visit, in my carry-on luggage. Most important of all was the collection of old photographs, especially those taken by Ernest Oberholtzer in 1912 of the Inuit he met at the mouth of the Thlewiaza, who were undoubtedly the ancestors of some people living in Arviat today.

It is twenty years since I was last in Arviat, back when it was still Eskimo Point, so the first impression that strikes my eyes from the air is that it has grown tremendously, as have all twenty-six Inuit communities scattered across the huge land mass that is now Nunavut, Canada's largest northern territory. The surface area of Nunavut is twice that of British Columbia and nearly three times the size of Texas. The distance from north to south, or east to west, across Nunavut is approximately 1,500 miles, roughly the distance from Minneapolis to either San Diego or Miami. When you land in Arviat, however, you are not yet quite halfway from the U.S. border to the very northern tip of Canada. There is a lot more to Canada's North than most people realize, both literally and figuratively.

Nunavut has been my stomping ground for thirty years, for both my professional research and writing, and for my favorite recreation, canoeing the barrenlands rivers. So despite not having been to Arviat for many years, I have friends and contacts there. One of them, a man I have admired deeply for many years, is waiting for me in the small airport as my plane touches down.

Luke Suluk has dedicated much of his life to the exploration and preservation of Inuit cultural heritage. He has worked out in the field with archaeologists and in his hometown with anthropologists. He has interviewed Inuit elders in his community about their early lives out on the land, including some who once lived and hunted the country surrounding Nueltin Lake and the Thlewiaza River. He has worked politically to ensure that all this documentation is properly protected for the benefit of future generations. His beaming smile and warm handshake await as I step into the small terminal—we are equally excited at the prospect of the next few days' discoveries.

∽ ∽ ∽ ∽ ∽

Although Inuit had been living along the Hudson Bay coast in the vicinity of Eskimo Point—hence the name given upon first encounter with the white man—it was not until the establishment of a Hudson's Bay Company post in 1921 that it became in any sense a community. The HBC was followed quickly by both the Roman Catholic and then the Anglican churches, the latter ultimately succeeding to the greater extent in this particular location.

When the Reverend Donald Marsh, a newly frocked Anglican missionary, arrived off the shore of Eskimo Point in an HBC schooner in August 1926, he wrote: "When the anchor dropped, against a background of conical skin tents I saw old men with long, flowing hair, smiling, wrinkled and seamed faces, clad in caribou skins so stained that many of them looked the color of the earth. They stooped slightly forward as they walked, as if to help themselves along, yet with the dignity and ease of men sure of themselves." In the following months, Marsh built the first Anglican mission at Eskimo Point, and in subsequent years he traveled

Eskimo Point (now Arviat) when it was little more than the Anglican mission beside a cluster of Hudson's Bay Company buildings, ca. 1930.

widely by dog team to visit the Inuit camps scattered across the interior stretching toward Nueltin Lake, Ennadai Lake, and the Kazan River. By his own account, his parish covered an area greater than fifty thousand square miles, the territory of the Padleimiut and the Ahiarmiut.

The first government school opened in Eskimo Point in 1959, and slowly thereafter the people moved into town from their camps on the land, hastened in many cases by a struggle to survive when the caribou seemed to disappear from the land. The settlement grew slowly into the thriving community it is today, with a current population of approximately two thousand. In the 1980s, it was a major center of Inuit cultural preservation and of efforts to invent new words in Inuktitut so the language would survive by embracing new inventions like computers and space shuttles. In 1988, the residents voted to change the community name to the more traditional designation Arviat, meaning Bowhead Whale Calf.

⌄   ⌄   ⌄   ⌄   ⌄

Suluk had spread word in advance of my arrival, so within the hour we were gathered in the community's heritage center with an energized group of seventeen Inuit elders, Oberholtzer's photographs spread out on a table, everyone staring in near disbelief at the images before them, talking excitedly. Round and round went the photos as one and then another of the elders examined each one in great detail, with memories stirred, long-departed faces remembered. There was much to be learned. Though no one had ever heard of Oberholtzer, they certainly knew—in some cases were related to—the Inuit family whom Oberholtzer met at the mouth of the Thlewiaza.

The man whose name Oberholtzer recorded as "Bite," which must have been an English nickname given by traders in Churchill, was in fact known by my group of informants as Ukkitaaq (Sharpshooter), though his real name, I learned, was Uturuuq. He was known by his nickname to such an extent that most people had

Oruluk, son of Ukkitaaq (Bite), as a young boy in 1912.
His descendants live today in Arviat.

forgotten his real name. Ukkitaaq's wife, who appears in one of Oberholtzer's photographs, was Tassiuq, whose name was recorded phonetically by Oberholtzer as "Tah-he-oh." They had three sons: Oruluk (Oberholtzer's "Oh-rut-yuk"), Apak, and Nauksauk, who may also appear in Oberholtzer's photographs.

Henry Isluanik, now in his eighties, remembered this family in his camp when he was a teenager, about 1940. By then, Ukkitaaq and his wife were among the older people in camp, and their sons had grown up. Isluanik produced a sketch map of the camp at a place called Tavani, showing his family's tent, Ukkitaaq's family's tent, other families' tents, some rough storehouses that had been erected, some graves, and the lay of the land, the coast, and the sea. Sometime about 1940, he recalled, the other families all moved south to the area closer to where Arviat is today.

The oldest among my informants, Richard Tutsweetuk, who himself could barely see or hear and whose family originated in the country surrounding the Thlewiaza, remembered that when

Ukkitaaq was an old man, his eyesight failing, he continued to hunt. According to Tutsweetuk, Ukkitaaq rigged his rifle with a special sight so he could see the caribou. And he remembered watching one time as Ukkitaaq used the rig to shoot a swan at Maguse Lake. Only Tutsweetuk remembered that Ukkitaaq's real name was Uturuuq.

Another elder at the table, Donald Uluadluk, seventy-five, remembered Ukkitaaq from the time near Arviat. Ukkitaaq had been accused of murdering a white trapper who had disappeared near Thlewiaza. It was nonsense, insisted Uluadluk. Ukkitaaq swore at the time that he had not killed the man, saying the trapper had gone crazy so that he had just decided to leave him alone at his camp. One time, said Uluadluk, "Ukkitaaq told us that he had dreamed something might happen to him, when we were all living near the narrows at Maguse Lake," not far from Arviat. "He said if something happened, that's where he wanted to be buried. Shortly after that, he died." Ukkitaaq is buried near Maguse Lake on the north side of the narrows, not far inland from present-day Arviat. These elders could lead me to his grave. He died, as did many others, during an epidemic that swept through the region in 1941. Both Uluadluk and Isluanik remember hearing old Ukkitaaq's songs, for which he was widely known, especially for one in particular about a crazy white trapper.

Ukkitaaq's son Oruluk, photographed by Oberholtzer as a young boy, later married a woman named Uttuk. Some of their children are elders in the community of Arviat today. Oruluk and Uttuk had a son whom they named Ukkitaaq, to carry on the name, who died young, at about thirty years of age. They had a daughter whom they named Tassiuq—Oruluk evidently wanted to honor both of his parents—who is alive today and nearly sixty years old. And there are others; in fact the descendants of Ukkitaaq were too numerous to count. Oruluk himself died in 1978.

It is in some small measure assumption, though highly likely, that the Inuk whom Norwegian adventurer Christian Leden met on this same stretch of Hudson Bay coast, whose name he recorded as "Beik," was in reality the same Ukkitaaq. When Leden traveled this region, with Inuit, just one year after Oberholtzer, he mentioned in his journal "the Eskimo, Beik, who sailed north from Churchill a few hours prior to our departure." Eleven days later, Leden's boat was shipwrecked, leaving him and his Inuit companions in dire straits on the storm-swept coast of Hudson Bay. They made camp in miserable conditions and survived on some rotting seal meat carried on the expedition for dog food until the weather permitted the Inuit to go hunting for caribou. Not long after, Beik arrived in camp "with five dogs harnessed to his komatik *[qamutik]*," headed north looking for caribou, and on his sled "his entire baggage amounts to a sleeping bag and a little skin tent." Leden was clearly impressed with the man, whom he described as "active and alert" and "an honourable and worthy man." Leden and his party eventually made their way back to Churchill, though not with ease. To be certain, without the Inuit, Leden himself would never have been seen again. Several weeks later, Leden recorded seeing Beik again, on his way in to trade at the HBC post. "He has a whole komatik load of fox pelts, which he got by the hundreds when he found them feeding on the carcass of the whale near the scene of our shipwreck. Now the time has come when he can buy tea and syrup and mouth organs for his children, while his wife can buy anything that her heart desires, including red handkerchiefs, beads and a pocket mirror." Ukkitaaq, it would seem, was an extraordinary person, even among his contemporaries. That it was this man whom Oberholtzer should happen to encounter at the mouth of the Thlewiaza appears to have been an unfathomable stroke of good luck.

Oberholtzer was equally impressed by the second man he met, Ahmak, who assisted "Bite" in sailing the boat to Churchill. Ahmak was Ukkitaaq's older brother. They had a third brother, named Apsaitok, whom Oberholtzer did not encounter, but whose son Oochupadlak (Oberholtzer's "Oo-too-pul-yak") does appear in the 1912 photographs. Both he and his cousin (not brother) Oruluk were young boys at the time but old enough to help with

Oochupadlak, though still a youth in 1912,
was an active helper for his two uncles Ukkitaaq and Ahmak.

the work in camp and on the boat. Ahmak was lost in a boating accident on October 10, 1949, when he and his son Nanauq, accompanied by Fr. Dion, became lost in fog and were never seen again. Oochupadlak, like his father before him, also died in an accident when his dogsled overturned in 1955.

For the elders gathered around the table, all of these stories came flooding back to life when they held in their hands the photographs taken by Oberholtzer in 1912. I left Arviat with a lasting image fixed in my mind of two older men, Luke Kinnisie and Leo Ahmak, seventy-four and sixty-two, respectively, staring in disbelief at an image of their long-departed grandfather, Ahmak. Through them, I had forged a palpable link back to the time of their grandfather, when Oberholtzer himself had encountered these Padleimiut.

Ahmak in 1912 (above) *has many descendants living today in Arviat, among them* (below) *Leo Ahmak* (left) *and his older brother, Luke Kinniksi, shown here in 2006 looking for the first time at a photo of their grandfather.*

Heading South

Before dawn on Sunday, September 22, 1912, it was raining heavily in Churchill. By noon, the rain had all but stopped, and the northwest wind was down to a gentle breeze. It was time to go. Oberholtzer and Magee said their farewells, and set off to canoe the 150-mile stretch of Hudson Bay coast between Churchill and York Factory. The major difficulties here rise and fall with the wind and the tide. It can blow for days, when the shallow inshore waters near the coast produce huge rollers that are only exacerbated by the tidal swings. There is always the danger of being swept out to sea on a falling tide or being stranded on an exposed tidal flat of mud several miles from the high-water mark. At the first long point east of Churchill, the two men pulled into shore to make camp before nightfall, relieved to be underway, but uneasy with the strange paddling conditions.

They did not move the next day. By Oberholtzer's account, "a heavy west wind kept [them] in camp all day," huddled by the fire, enduring "flurries of hail and snow." On Tuesday, determined to advance, they paddled across the small bay in front of their camp, intending to portage over the long point and continue on.

▷ ▷ *A rising wind, however, discouraged us from trying to go farther. After waiting an hour in the wind, we made our beds under the canoe and started a fire among the rocks. The sky again looked dark and threatening and the tide came in as rough as ever.*

On Wednesday, the weather gods smiled, delivering "a calm sea and intermittent breezes" under an overcast sky. The two paddled for ten hours without touching land and then made camp.

Thursday and Friday they were windbound. On Saturday morning they again set off.

▷ ▷ *Launched the canoe on the breakers at eight o'clock and paddled on a heavy sea for two hours. As the tide turned, the west wind seemed to strengthen. We came to a long point where the waves were spouting over the reefs for a mile out like volcanoes. We hardly dared go outside and the beach looked too rough for a landing. At last, after a big wave went down my neck, we paddled straight for shore and were thrown high up on the sand beach.*

At this point, Oberholtzer began to contemplate paddling at night. Fortunately, Magee resisted. Without good visibility, given the ever-present possibility of a sudden increase in the wind and the difficulty of remaining close to shore as the tide falls, paddling at night could easily be the added element of danger to push the canoeists over the edge. Their caution was rewarded. The next day dawned "fair and balmy," so the canoe was launched. By nine in the morning, they were "paddling on a glassy sea" in rare, warm sunshine. They pushed ahead for thirteen and a half hours, until well after a glorious sunset. By ten o'clock the next morning, they were back on the water, this time with a following wind that allowed them to hoist a sail. "Go some now," said Magee, as they surged forward "at a very merry clip." Fourteen hours and about fifty miles later, they made camp by the mouth of a broad river.

Tuesday, October 1, was spent resting in camp in anticipation of a night paddle. Just before dawn the next morning, Oberholtzer leaned over the side of their canoe and with his hand scooped some water up to his mouth. "To my delight, it was fresh." They were paddling in the mouth of the Nelson River. Many years later, Oberholtzer recalled the scene.

"You taste the water," I said [to Billy]. It was fresh water. So he takes his paddle and drips it in his mouth, and he could taste that too, fresh water. Then I thought, well, now my time [to tell Billy] has come. "Now," I said, "Billy—of course I was overjoyed—you know what that water is you drank? That's Tchi-ma-og'-ane' River." That's water that came from Seine River. So he knew—that came from his home. He knew instantly what that meant. He didn't know the name of that river, but he knew that it connected with his home, you see.

York Factory is situated on the long peninsula formed by the two major rivers that enter Hudson Bay side by side at this point, the Nelson and the Hayes. Late in the day on October 3, after overcoming some final frustrations, Oberholtzer stepped ashore in front of the old HBC post.

▷ ▷ *At the fort I went straight over the hill to Mr. Ray's house. When I knocked, a whole company of men filed out of the door. Mr. Ray* was last, as much bewildered when I handed him the letters from Churchill as I was by all the strange faces. Soon I was eating fried trout and tea and cakes and butter and all sorts of delicacies. Then I got Billy in a tent with some Indians, changed my clothes, and spent the evening telling the company in the billiard room about my trip. I had a kind and appreciative audience.*

⌣   ⌣   ⌣   ⌣   ⌣

The best, more or less contemporaneous description of York Factory came from an Anglican missionary, Reverend John Lofthouse. He himself was a prodigious traveler who, in his own words, "thought no more of a walk of 200 miles than of one of 20 in the Old Country." In the years just before Oberholtzer's arrival, Lofthouse had canoed in similar country northwest of Churchill, which experience later led to the two men's conferring on their respective routes. Writing some years later, he remembered the scene at York Factory when he first arrived there by sea from England in October 1883.

York Fort, or Factory, as it is more generally called, situated on the Hayes River about four miles from its junction with the

* George R. Ray was the post manager.

Nelson, has, ever since the formation of the Hudson's Bay Company in 1670, been one of their most important posts, expecially so before the opening of the Canadian Pacific Railway, when it was the depot for the whole western country, and the York boats came here not only from Fort Frances, Winnipeg, and the surrounding country, but from Edmonton and the faraway Mackenzie River. . . .

The arrival of the annual ship at York was the great event of the year, and might take place any time between the middle of August and the end of September, according to the state of the ice in the Strait and the Bay. At that time forty or fifty chief factors, factors, chief traders, and traders would assemble at York from all parts to obtain their yearly supplies and to send home to England the furs they had collected during the winter. Then, indeed, it was a busy scene on the banks of the Hayes.

The present fort is only one left of the three or four that were built by the Company on the swampy land forming the peninsula between the Hayes and Nelson Rivers, and either abandoned because of their unsanitary position or burnt down. It is stockaded, as was usual with all their forts, and boasts, or rather did boast in 1883, six large gateways which were all closed and locked at dark. The large storehouse which stands in the centre is one of the finest buildings in the Hudson's Bay regions, and is capable of containing supplies for the whole of the trading posts.

At one time a staff of twenty clerks and nearly one hundred men, coopers, tinsmiths, boat-builders, and carpenters, were in regular employment, and in summer nearly all the Indians were also employed.

York Factory was the first, and for many years the sole, HBC post for the western fur trade. Once the Company began to establish posts in the interior, York Factory served increasingly as a depot, as the point of transshipment for furs headed to England and trade goods arriving from England on the annual ship. The actual buildings varied, and the site was moved several times within the peninsula. The French twice captured the fort, in1697 and 1782, but on both occasions it reverted to the British. It closed in 1957, and today there are no permanent residents, though the remaining historic buildings have been preserved.

Robert Ballantyne, an ʜʙᴄ clerk who arrived at York Factory by sea, at age sixteen in 1841, described his first sight of North America this way:

> York Factory is the principal depôt of the Northern department, from whence all the supplies for the trade are issued, and where all the returns of the department are collected and shipped for England. As may be supposed, then, the establishment is a large one. There are always between thirty and forty men resident at the post, summer and winter; generally four or five clerks, a postmaster, and a skipper for the small schooners; and the whole is under direction and superintendence of a chief factor, or chief trader.

At the time of Oberholtzer's brief visit in 1912, a beaver pelt was worth about four dollars* and could be traded for seventy sticks of plug tobacco, eighty boxes of waxed and waterproofed matches, or corresponding amounts of sugar, calico, rifles, ammunition, and other popular items. The Cree word for York Factory is Kitchi-waskiegan, meaning the Great House, which refers to the main depot building, an impressive three-story structure with a look-out tower on the top used to search for the arriving supply ships. In the early twentieth century, local Cree were employed at York Factory in all manner of labor: cutting hay, cutting firewood, hunting for food, and so on. It was still a busy place, perched at the mouth of the Hayes River, a waterway of immense significance in the history of the fur trade. Though the point was certainly not lost on Oberholtzer, given his sense of history, he made only one relevant—and rather comical—note in the back of his journal.

▷ ▷ *York boats from all parts of the country used to separate on Lake Winnipeg. Once on the way from York the man with the rum barrel dropped it on a bare rock portage. Forthwith every man lay down on the rock and there they stayed for two days.*

As Oberholtzer prepared to follow a small brigade of York boats heading upriver to Oxford House, he was in effect about to follow

* In 1912, Cdn$4 would have been equivalent to Cdn$74 in 2007.

in the wake of a fur trade tradition that stretched back through time. For more than a hundred years, HBC men had been heading inland in pursuit of furs, up this river. Since merging with the North West Company, the HBC had used York boats on the Hayes River to supply the interior network of trading posts. This was a river with history.

⌄   ⌄   ⌄   ⌄   ⌄

The HBC post manager's journal for October 4, 1912, states simply: "Cold and miserable. Mr. Overholtzer [sic] left this forenoon by canoe for Oxford. He will get the Oxford men to help him on his way." In reality, Oberholtzer accepted the "help" somewhat reluctantly.

◊ ◊ *Nothing would do, according to all the men at the fort, but that I must go back to Oxford House with the same Indians that had brought down the last party. The leader of the Indians said I might get drowned on the rapids and all the white men as usual were sure I would get lost. Much as I disliked tying myself to the Indians, I had to dicker with them till they agreed to take some of my packs and to see me safely over the rapids for $2.00 apiece. They were very impatient to be off and I was not nearly ready.*

The earlier fur trade clerk, Robert Ballantyne, left us an apt description of the river at this time of year.

> As the season advanced, the days became shorter and the nights more frosty; and soon a few flakes of snow began to fall, indicating the approach of winter. About the beginning of October the cold damp snowy weather that usually precedes winter set in; and shortly after Hayes River was full of drifting ice, and the whole country covered with snow. A week or so after this, the river was completely frozen over; and Hudson's Bay itself, as far as the eye could reach, was covered with a coat of ice.

Ideal conditions for travel by canoe, it was not. Magee and Oberholtzer tried tracking the canoe upstream, the technique used by the local Cree river-men, who had perfected it to an art. For the uninitiated, however, it was not easy, and the two weary travelers soon gave up and reverted to their paddles, aided by a following wind. They were, as it turned out in these favorable conditions, able to match, and even surpass on occasion, the progress of the men from Oxford House.

The Cree technique for tracking was described by another southern canoeist who had paddled down—and tracked back up— the Hayes River in 1911. In his trip journal, Kenneth Campbell, a dentist from Winnipeg who did the trip with three friends and four Cree guides, wrote:

> This tracking is great business. The tracking line is 180 ft. long, about 170 ft. is normally used, except when the canoe has to go out far to avoid shallow water, and the full length is used. The line is ¼" thick and is tied to the 1st. thwart of the canoe. In order to make the stern run easily the painter is tied to the line and drawn up a little. The man steering the canoe ordinarily keeps it out about 30 or 40 ft. The bowman keeps on the look-out to see that the line doesn't catch on snags. The two men pulling have "tump lines" (used for portaging loads on one's back) tied to the tracking line which is placed across the chest—over one shoulder and under the other arm—so that the arms and hands are free. Sometimes we hauled at the water's edge, sometimes on top of a bank and other times half way up on a steep bank where the footing is insecure. We struggled over gravel, rocks, sand, mud and blue clay and through bushes and long grasses—all kinds of tracking in all kinds of weather.

For the next week, the two parties paddled steadily upstream, Oberholtzer matching the Cree's pace, though not without considerable effort. They were greeted every morning by frost and often had to break a rim of ice on the river in order to launch the canoe. Occasionally, the Cree party helped carry their packs around a portage and offered the men caribou or moose to eat, so their company certainly held some advantage. On Sunday, October 13, the expanded party pulled up onto the beach at Oxford House after nine days of hard upstream travel. Oberholtzer was determined, however, to keep going, anxious to get home and concerned about the advancing season.

▷ ▷ *Mr. Bayer* of the Company and his assistant, Mr. Cran, came down to meet us. Bayer gruffly informed me that I would not get through to Norway House before winter and then when he found that I had my own Indian and would not become a burdensome guest invited me up to the house. There his Indian wife prepared Billy and me a lunch. I paid Mr. Cran $2.50 a piece for my men or $15.00 in all and $0.75 for 5 pounds of beans. As soon as Johnie had told Billy how to go down the lake the 34 mile stretch to the river, I started off again, hoping to reach Norway House on the 17th. Camped at half past five on fine little point ten miles or so from the fort.*

He paid the Cree men something, despite being told by the post manager that "they told [him] they don't want anything. The old fellow [Johnie] says in all his years he's never seen anybody paddle up the Hayes River before."

Relying on advice from Cree camps along the way and "a descriptive map on a scale of 25 miles to the inch in the booklet that the police at Churchill gave me," Oberholtzer struggled on toward Norway House where, he hoped, they could catch the last steamer of the season, heading south across Lake Winnipeg. The morning of October 19, at the outskirts of Norway House—the biggest center the two men had seen in months—Oberholtzer "shaved and put on clean clothes" before paddling in to meet the teacher and the Company men.

Norway House had been central during the heyday of the fur trade in the nineteenth century, given its strategic location. This was the head of the transportation corridor from York Factory on Hudson Bay, up the Hayes River, to the interior. From Norway

* Raymond T. Bayer was later post manager at Norway House and, subsequently, an independent trader.

House trade goods were distributed to the network of trading posts to the northwest. Even after the Canadian Pacific Railway was built, permitting goods to be shipped west by train from Montreal to Winnipeg, steamboats carried the trading supplies across Lake Winnipeg to Norway House for onward distribution. During their brief stop there, Oberholtzer bought eight pounds of pork, two packets of dates, one jar of jam, and one small can of baking powder, for three dollars. All this was necessary because they had missed the last boat of the season by two days.

The last leg of their journey, down the western shore of Lake Winnipeg, was extremely difficult, especially given the late season. At any time of year, this is not ideal water for canoeing. The lake's expanse encouraged unimpeded winds. The freezing temperatures of late October and early November made conditions that much more severe for Oberholtzer and Magee. "The wind was northeast and paddling in the driving snow was far from comfortable." For four days straight they were windbound on the lee shore of Lake Winnipeg. Gale-force winds visited them with regularity, often from the northwest, effectively pinning them down in camp on the exposed eastern shore. On the rare days when weather permitted, they paddled and sailed slowly south. Ice was forming along the fringe of the lake. "The water froze in my coat and gloves as fast as it sprayed."

On Tuesday, November 5, as if it were just another day not unlike the 132 that preceded it along the way, Oberholtzer recorded in his journal what should have been a crowning moment.

▷ ▷ *Weather warmer and lake calm. At half past nine in clear sunlight we started again. Fishermen putting out in their boats all along the shore. A light variable wind. Reached point near Gimli [a town and railhead] at half past one o'clock and Billy cooked lunch while I walked into town to send a telegram.*

Their long journey by canoe, two thousand miles from start to finish, was at an end.

The Outside

▷ ▷ *Nov. 8. Registered at the Ryan Hotel, St. Paul. Wired Associated Press and received negative reply about my story.*

Within three days of their arrival in Gimli, on the ice-clad shores of Lake Winnipeg, the two men had had haircuts, baths, and a couple nights' sleep in hotel beds and were returned to their respective homes to the south, traveling swiftly by rail. It seems an anticlimactic end to what must be considered an epic journey: 2,000 miles in 133 days, by canoe.

On Oberholtzer's first full day back in the United States, his story received its first rejection. He says nothing of how he felt. Here was a man who set himself a goal, with explicit guidelines, in his notebook while planning the trip. "Real stories full of zest, reality, daring, reckless, resourceful, wonderful—let the reader draw breath at the end and exclaim 'But he was a man.' Tell it cold-bloodedly, off-hand, so that it allows a picture of truth." That he wanted to write about the expedition into "the vast unknown North" cannot be questioned. Writing represented a lifestyle, an image, and recognition, all of which he desired at some point. "I thought, well, there are probably other groups of those Eskimos up in there. What that would mean, what a delight to be the first one ever to find them!!"

Not quite two weeks later, on November 20, the trip achieved a touch of notoriety when an article appeared in the *Evening Citizen*, in Ottawa. Of the Thlewiaza portion of Oberholtzer and Magee's trip, it reads, "For 400 miles the route was where no white man had ever been." These words must have seemed music to Oberholtzer's ears. "No such trip has been known to be accomplished by two men and a single canoe, and many escapes from disaster were experienced."

In a letter that winter, Oberholtzer expressed confidence. "I am writing up a long narrative of the trip and feel sure I can get it published—only the returns are in doubt. I have some fine material." In fact, he never produced such a narrative, and no full account of his journey was ever published by him. Many years later, in 1964, when he was eighty, the desire to write up the "Hudson Bay trip" lingered. He told a researcher then that "If I don't do anything else, I would like to do that. But now I realize that I haven't very much time. I would like to at least do that, you see." He never did, though he lived until 1977.

⌣ ⌣ ⌣ ⌣ ⌣

In the winter of 1912 to 1913, Oberholtzer set to work most immediately to produce a sketch map of the previously uncharted portion of his trip, Nueltin and the Thlewiaza. Over the winter and through most of the next year, the details of this map occupied much of his attention. The logic is self-evident. If he were to be perceived as an explorer, he would have to produce a map of his "discoveries."

Within days of his return home, Oberholtzer wrote a letter to his hero J. B. Tyrrell reporting on the journey and raising the matter of his own survey work, which began in earnest at the point (Theitaga, now Kasmere Lake) where his route diverged from Tyrrell's 1894 trip to the Kazan. "From there to the sea I made a rough sketch map, which is at least accurate enough to prevent future travelers from paddling into wrong bays of lakes." It is apparent in the letter that he hopes to engage in a discussion befitting two explorers sharing their insights.

Tyrrell wrote back by return post, with polite and encouraging words, suggesting that Samuel Hearne and Reverend Lofthouse were probably the only predecessors on the Thlewiaza. "I shall look with much interest to seeing your account of your whole trip, and especially of that portion of it which was through absolutely new country, and the sketch that you made of the route, and I heartily congratulate you on having made a good adventurous journey which will add materially to our knowledge of that portion of Northern Canada." Of greatest immediate concern to Oberholtzer was establishing with certainty where he had arrived on the coast of Hudson Bay, at the river mouth where he encountered Bite. Following on the implicit suggestion from J. B. Tyrrell, he pursued an extensive discussion with Lofthouse about the Hudson Bay coast and the various rivers that descend to it in the vicinity of Thlewiaza. The missionary had traveled inland on the Tha-Anne River in 1896.* Several letters were exchanged. Lofthouse was convinced that it could not have been the Thlewiaza that Oberholtzer descended. Although Oberholtzer's mapping was imperfect—as tools, he had only his "a dollar and half watch and a dollar and a half compass, for finding [his] way and mapping the country," and an ability to estimate distances—he *had* correctly identified and placed the river. It was most certainly the Thlewiaza, not the Maguse or Ferguson farther north, as Lofthouse suggested.

Nonetheless, he was unable to sell his maps with the geographical descriptions of his observations.† The government of Canada, while commending his effort, indicated that "the information contained in the report is not such as would be of practical use to us in connection with the preparation of our official maps" and offered only to keep his report on file for possible future use. They offered no remuneration whatsoever. Another aspect of his dreams was apparently dashed.

❧   ❧   ❧   ❧   ❧

By his own account, Oberholtzer was too busy, always "eager to experience" life, to spend time writing about what had already happened. But that did not stop him from reliving his experi-

---

* The Tha-Anne is, in fact, the next river to the north of the Thlewiaza and empties into Hudson Bay in the same small bay along the coast, but neither man was clear on this at the time.

† The twenty-one-page document, entitled "Description of Canoe Route—Thlewiaza River from Theitaga Lake to Hudson Bay, to Accompany Sketch Map," is still extant in the archives of the Minnesota Historical Society, as is the map itself.

ences; in that, he took great pleasure, and no experience was more important to his oral storytelling than the Hudson Bay trip. In much the same vein, it was particularly exciting for him when he made contact with P. G. Downes, the canoeist who had followed his route north from Brochet up to Nueltin in 1939. In Downes's diary, after meeting the old trapper Cecil "Husky" Harris in Churchill, he wrote, "Harris tells me that Oberhauser, or Oben-hauser, made his trip through in 1911." Downes knew he wanted to meet this man, his predecessor. Oberholtzer himself recounted how this happened several years after the fact.

> [Downes] went home, and he inquired everywhere to try to get some idea of who this man was, you see, who had been there long before. He was in the habit of buying books on wilderness and exploration. It was getting near Christmas, and he went in a bookshop, and he saw a book, *A New Life of Daniel Boone*, by a man named John Bakeless, who lives near New York and who knew me very well and had been up at my place many times, taking canoe trips that we had planned for him, and who had written many, many books. He'd written this life of Boone. The best ever done, a fine study. He was a very thorough scholar. He'd written this, and sent me a copy of it at Christmas. And to my astonishment, when I had opened it to the title page, I saw that it said: "To Ernest C. Oberholtzer, a modern master of the wilderness." Well, I was tremendously complimented, and I knew it wasn't just—but just the same you could appreciate the compliment. And when I saw it, I thought to myself, why, did he really go to the trouble of having each one of these books inscribed with the name of the friend he's giving it to this Christmas. Then I just began to tumble. Why, he's actually dedicated that book to me, you see. I didn't know he was going to do it.
>
> But, anyway, this man who'd been up in the barrenlands found that book in the bookshop, and he thought, why that sounds like that fellow the priest [Fr. Egenolf at Brochet] told me about. So he wrote to the publishers, and asked, could you give me John Bakeless's address, which they were glad to do. And he wrote John Bakeless and said, "Did your friend Ober-holtzer ever go up into the barrenlands?" "Well, I should say he

did," Bakeless said. So then he wrote me one of the finest letters I've ever received in my life.

In their correspondence Oberholtzer and Downes compared notes, reminisced, and generally reveled in the shared spirit of companions on the trail. As Downes said, "It is a little like the trappers and all the northern men who spend so much time when they are 'in' talking about what they will do when they get 'outside' and when they do go 'outside' they all congregate at the same hotel and sit around and talk about the north." Downes was able to update Oberholtzer on developments in the North in the nearly thirty years since the older man had made his trip. They congratulated each other on being "the only two who have penetrated to and through Nueltin," though that necessarily ignores the Dene, the Inuit, the traders, and the trappers. They were to that point, however, the only two canoeists, which had its own cachet. Downes proposed that "as we two seem to be about the only living whitemen to have set a canoe in mighty Nueltin, I believe that every effort should be made to have a meeting." This they did when Downes and his new wife visited Oberholtzer shortly thereafter.

P. G. Downes, of course, did publish a compelling narrative of his travels following the old way north.* In a letter to Oberholtzer in July 1941, he said, "At the time of your letter's arrival I was working over an account of my own wanderings in the Nueltin Lake country; trying to get together some sort of a manuscript affair about the trip and the region both of which are by far the most interesting to me of my own small experiences in the North."† Three years later, in 1944, after the book's publication, when Oberholtzer wrote expressing his "pleasure" upon reading it, Downes

---

* A marvelous account of his travels by canoe up to the Nueltin Lake country, *Sleeping Island*, was published in 1943.

† Downes was in fact quite widely traveled in the North, having been to the Mackenzie Valley, the Great Bear and Great Slave lakes, Bellot Strait at the top of the Boothia, Ellesmere Island, Baffin Island, and around the northern tip of Labrador by sea and to many points in between.

replied, saying, "There are many things now I wish I had put in the book—it was published when I was up to my ears here—and I couldn't find time to even read the proofs. . . . The war is so all-demanding for me that I unhappily find much of those happy days fading from my mind too fast for comfort."

Downes left a literary legacy that surpasses anything Oberholtzer was likely to produce but serves well to memorialize the time and place through which they both traveled. It seems probable that Oberholtzer recognized this. As he explained it to Downes, "I have never published anything about this trip. It was my ambition at the time to return to the general locality for five years, but that could never be carried out and my life has been very crowded ever since."

⌄ ⌄ ⌄ ⌄ ⌄

Although Oberholtzer was not to become the prolific author he had once imagined, telling "real stories full of zest," his epic journey to Hudson Bay, following the old way north into the deepest wilderness of "the vast unknown," did have a lasting and profound impact on the rest of his life. Writing for publication, and for recognition, became less important to him, perhaps in part because of the wilderness experience and the opportunity for self-examination that it afforded. On some level, within his own psyche, Oberholtzer allowed this expedition to define his identity for the rest of his life. Though he never wrote about it substantially, neither did he let the experience die. It empowered him by allowing him to believe he had experienced a certain union with the wilderness. The very fact that he had accomplished the journey gave him the confidence to undertake other less physical but nevertheless important wilderness projects.

One biographer wrote that Oberholtzer was "the central figure in the seemingly endless struggle to preserve the wilderness areas on the Minnesota-Ontario border" and "one of the prime movers for the establishment of the Boundary Waters Canoe Area." All of this—his life's work, really*—might well not have happened had Oberholtzer not undertaken as a young man in his twenties to paddle his canoe north to Hudson Bay and back.

▽ ▽ ▽ ▽ ▽

When Ernest Oberholtzer followed the old way north from Brochet to Nueltin, it was a veritable highway. Hunters and trappers headed north in pursuit of their way of life, and freighters moved trade goods north bound for the numerous posts scattered through the Country. Meat and furs came south. Brochet was a center of commerce. The Dene whom Oberholtzer met in town and along the trail were people attached to the land in the deepest sense.

Alphonse Dzeylion, whom Oberholtzer met in Brochet, had he been hired as a guide, would have provided such a different experience of the Thlewiaza. Traveling upriver on the Cochrane, Oberholtzer encountered a group of Dene heading south to Brochet to trade, twenty men and boys in five canoes and their chief, likely Casimir. A few days later Oberholtzer paddled through the narrows where Casimir asked to be buried, on a hillside, so he could watch over his land and his people. Just north of this future gravesite, Oberholtzer passed the small fur trade post of Redhead, one of the most influential leaders in recent Dene history. These are in reality remarkable contacts with the traditional Dene society that were, for Oberholtzer himself, little more than passing incidents. He was on a quest of a different sort. In 1912, the lives of the Dene had changed little for several centuries, but change was imminent. Caribou was still central to their lives; elders said they followed the herds like the wolves. Oberholtzer witnessed this old way of life, however incidentally; thus his trip offers us a glimpse into the past.

Earlier in his trip, farther south, he had followed the old routes of the fur trade: The Pas, Saskatchewan River, Cumberland House,

* For a full account of Oberholtzer's life's work, read the excellent biography *Keeper of the Wild*, by Joe Paddock.

Pelican Narrows, Churchill River, and north to Reindeer Lake. Oberholtzer and Magee became part of the summer's bustle of the fur trade, where the fabric of society was woven of HBC factors and missionaries, York boat men and Cree freighters, and all the talk was of the North. It fueled Oberholtzer's imagination even as he traveled, just as it fuels ours today, looking back.

The two men successfully completed their journey—their quest to "go end earth"—and its personal impact was lifelong, no doubt. Seen from today's perspective, they were but shadows passing over the land, past its people and through its history. The lasting impression, surely, is the view to be gained by looking beyond their horizon, to see not only what they saw, and those they met, but likewise those who preceded them, as they followed the old way north, and by listening to the stories the land has to tell.

Envoi

In Canada, history is directly a function of our geography. Nowhere is this more evident than in an examination of the fur trade or of the coincidental travel by canoe on the interior waterways of this vast country. Many observers before me have commented on the Canadian reality that you can launch a canoe into Atlantic salt water and set out to paddle to either the Arctic Ocean or the Pacific Ocean without being overly concerned about lengthy portages. Sheer distance and climate might provide insurmountable hurdles, but either journey could be completed without having to resort to any excessively long walks. Such is the remarkable network of rivers and lakes that weave together our land; the rivers are the threads that tie our geography together. And much of our history results from this very fact, though much of it is relatively un-celebrated. Mounties, missionaries, fur traders, geologists, map-makers, explorers, and, before all of them, the Native people all used these waterways.

And few were used more than the old way north, the travel corridor into what remains today the heart of Canada's northern wilderness, from Manitoba to the vast stretch of Nunavut on the west side of Hudson Bay. That this small piece of history is now recorded in some measure is satisfying. More important, to me, is the illustration of the drama and the sense of national identity that the geography lends to our history.

Selected Bibliography

Ballantyne, Robert M. *Hudson's Bay, or Every-day Life in the Wilds of North America*. Edmonton, Alberta: Hurtig Publishers, 1972.

Borthwick, Thomas A. "Report of Second Commission for Treaty No. 10." Ottawa, Ontario: Department of Indian Affairs, 1907.

Buchanan, Captain Angus. *Wild Life in Canada*. Toronto, Ontario: McClelland, Goodchild and Stewart, 1920.

Campbell, K. C. "By Canoe to York Factory, Summer, 1911." *The Beaver*, August/September 1992, 19–35.

Christensen, Deanna. "Steamboat Bill of Cumberland House." *The Beaver*, Winter 1974, 28–31.

Cockburn, Robert H. "North of Reindeer: The 1940 Trip Journal of Prentice G. Downes." *The Beaver*, Spring 1983, 36–43.

———. "Voyage to Nutheltin." *The Beaver*, January/February 1986, 4–27.

———. "After-Images of Rupert's Land from the Journals of Ernest Oberholtzer (1912) and P. G. Downes (1939)." In *Rupert's Land: A Cultural Tapestry*, edited by Richard C. Davis, 275–97. Waterloo, Ontario: Wilfred Laurier University Press, 1988.

Downes, Prentice G. *Sleeping Island*. New York: Coward-McCann, 1943.

Duchaussois, Reverend P. *Mid Snow and Ice: The Apostles of the North-West*. London: Burns, Oates and Washbourne, 1923.

Dunning, Gerry. *When the Foxes Ran*. Privately printed, n.d.

Gasté, Father Alphonse. "Father Gasté Meets the Inland Eskimos." *Eskimo* 57 (1960).

Gillespie, B. C. "Territorial Expansion of the Chipewyan in the 18th Century." In *Proceedings: Northern Athapaskan Conference, 1971*, edited by A. M. Clark. Mercury Series 27. Ottawa, Ontario: National Museum of Man, 1975.

———. "Changes in Territory and Technology of the Chipewyan." *Arctic Anthropology* 13, no. 1 (1976): 6–11.

Gordon, B. H. C. *Of Men and Herds in Barrenland Prehistory*. Mercury Series 28. Ottawa, Ontario: National Museum of Man, 1975.

Hearne, Samuel. *A Journey to the Northern Ocean*. Toronto, Ontario: MacMillan, 1958.

Helm, June. "Introduction to the Contact History of the Subarctic Athapaskans: An Overview." In *Proceedings: Northern Athapaskan Conference, 1971*, edited by A. M. Clark. Mercury Series 27. Ottawa, Ontario: National Museum of Man, 1975.

———. "Matonabbee's Map." *Arctic Anthropology* 26, no. 2 (1989): 28–47.

Holland, Lynda, and Mary Ann Kailther, eds. *They Will Have Our Words: The Dene Elders Project.* 2 vols. La Ronge, Saskatchewan: Holland-Dalby Educational Consulting, 2002–3.

Hudson's Bay Company. Post journals for various years from Lac du Brochet, Nueltin Lake, The Pas, Pelican Narrows, Cumberland House, York Factory, Oxford House, and Churchill. Hudson's Bay Company Archives.

Jan, Arthur J. "Memoirs of Fifty-six Years in Canada." Unpublished manuscript, 1964.

Keighley, Sydney A. *Trader, Tripper, Trapper: The Life of a Bay Man.* Winnipeg, Manitoba: Watson and Dwyer Publishing, 1989.

Lofthouse, Reverend Joseph. *A Thousand Miles from a Post Office.* London: Society for Promoting Christian Knowledge, 1922.

Lowery, R. "Ragnar Jonsson: Wilderness Master." In *The Unbeatable Breed: People and Events in Northern Manitoba.* Humboldt, Saskatchewan: Prairie Publishing, 1981.

Mallet, Captain Thierry. *Glimpses of the Barren Lands.* New York: Revillon Frères, 1930.

Martyn, Katharine. *J. B. Tyrrell: Explorer and Adventurer.* Toronto, Ontario: University of Toronto Library, 1993.

Paddock, Joe. *Keeper of the Wild: The Life of Ernest Oberholtzer.* St. Paul: Minnesota Historical Society Press, 2001.

Pelly, David F., and Christopher C. Hanks, eds. *The Kazan: Journey into an Emerging Land.* Yellowknife, Northwest Territories: Outcrop, 1991.

Petch, Virginia. "The Life Story of Charlie H. Schweder, Whose Heart and Soul Knew No Boundaries." Privately published, 1996.

Smith, J., and E. Burch Jr. "Chipewyan and Inuit in the Central Canadian Subarctic, 1613–1977." *Arctic Anthropology* 16, no. 2 (1979): 76–101.

Turquetil, Father Arsène. "The Second Journey of Fr. Turquetil to the Inuit (1906)." *Eskimo* 31 and 32 (1986).

Tyrrell, J. B. *Report of the Doobaunt, Kazan and Ferguson Rivers and the Northwest Coast of Hudson Bay.* Ottawa, Ontario: Annual Report of the Geological Survey, 1898.

Wokes, L., and Greg Thomas, eds. "An Interview with Moses Neepin." *Manitoba History* 5 (1983).

Yerbury, J. C. *The Subarctic Indians and the Fur Trade, 1680–1860.* Vancouver: University of British Columbia Press, 1986.

Index

PHOTO CREDITS

pages 38, 99, 152, 154, 163, 166, 167 (top): Ernest C. Oberholtzer, © 2008 the Ernest C. Oberholtzer Foundation

pages 76, 116, 118, 120, 121, 167 (bottom): photos by and courtesy of the author

pages 92, 110, 134, 145, 148: photos by and courtesy of Bill Layman

pages 11, 59: J. B. Tyrrell Collection, Thomas Fisher Rare Book Library, University of Toronto

page 4: unknown photographer, © 2008 the Ernest C. Oberholtzer Foundation

page 47: Archives Deschâtelets, Ottawa, Canada

page 57: James McDougall, Hudson's Bay Company Archives, Archives of Manitoba

page 73: C. S. MacDonald, Library and Archives Canada

page 161: Donald B. Marsh, Library and Archives Canada

The Old Way North
was designed and set in type by Will Powers
at the Minnesota Historical Society Press.
The text type is Miller Roman, designed by Matthew Carter.
Printed by Thomson-Shore, Inc., Dexter, Michigan.

Printed in the USA
CPSIA information can be obtained
at www.ICGtesting.com
LVHW040928150824
788261LV00004B/32